POSITIVITY

Pathway to
EMOTIONAL INTELLIGENCE

______________By______________

Joseph Anand

Table of Contents

Foreword

Why Positivity Matters Now

We are living in a time of unprecedented capability and unprecedented emotional strain. Never before have human beings had access to so much information, opportunity, and connectivity—yet rarely have so many people felt internally pressured, emotionally depleted, and mentally fragmented.

Speed has become the dominant currency of modern life. Decisions are expected quickly. Responses are demanded instantly. Comparison is constant and often invisible, shaping self-worth through metrics, performance, and social signals. In this environment, emotional vigilance is no longer an occasional response to threat—it has become a background condition.

This emotional climate has consequences.

When the inner world is dominated by urgency, defensiveness, or exhaustion, intelligence narrows. People may remain capable, informed, and technically skilled, yet find themselves reacting rather than responding, managing impressions rather than engaging authentically, and surviving demands rather than living with clarity and purpose.

This is why positivity matters now.

Not positivity as optimism, cheerfulness, or motivational enthusiasm—but positivity as an **inner emotional orientation**. A way of meeting life that remains open, constructive, and aligned, even when circumstances are complex or demanding.

Positivity, in this sense, is not a feeling to chase or perform. It is a condition that allows human intelligence—emotional, social, and moral—to function.

Modern culture has a complicated relationship with positivity. On one hand, it is often oversold as a cure-all, reduced to slogans, affirmations, or forced attitudes that deny pain and complexity. On the other hand, it is increasingly dismissed by serious thinkers as naïve or unrealistic. The result is a quiet abandonment of positivity altogether - replaced by emotional contraction disguised as realism.

This book takes a different position.

It recognizes that without a positive inner orientation, emotional intelligence becomes brittle. Awareness turns into self-criticism. Regulation becomes suppression. Empathy becomes draining. Motivation becomes pressure. Intelligence does not disappear—it loses the emotional environment it requires to operate.

Positivity, as explored here, is not about avoiding difficulty. It is about sustaining inner openness in the presence of difficulty. It is the difference between responding from capacity rather than from threat. Between engaging thoughtfully rather than defensively. Between navigating complexity with discernment rather than reactivity.

At a time when stress is normalized, emotional fatigue is widespread, and negativity quietly shapes behavior across workplaces, relationships, and societies, positivity is no longer optional. It is the pathway through which emotional intelligence becomes accessible, sustainable, and humane.

The pages that follow invite a re-examination of what it means to be emotionally intelligent in the modern world. They offer not techniques to master, but a deeper understanding of the emotional ground from which intelligence emerges.

In choosing positivity—not as performance, but as orientation—we choose the conditions in which clarity, empathy, and wisdom can take root again.

Dedication

This book is dedicated to the people who taught me that positivity is not an attitude we adopt, but a way of meeting life.

To my late wife, **Bibiana - —**

You showed me that emotional intelligence is not something we practice when life is easy, but something we embody when life is uncertain. Your presence carried a quiet positivity that neither denied difficulty nor hardened against it. In your listening, people felt safe. In your patience, urgency softened. You lived with an inner openness that allowed wisdom to emerge naturally, without force or display. Though you are no longer here in form, the emotional ground you stood on continues to guide my own. This book follows the pathway you lived.

To my children, **Desmond and Cynthia** -

You taught me that positivity is sustained not through control, but through relationship. Through loss, transition, and growth, you reminded me that staying open is an act of courage. Your trust, your steadiness, and your willingness to walk alongside me as I learned reshaped my understanding of emotional intelligence—not as strength alone, but as resilience with heart. This book exists because of you, and for you.

To the teachers, mentors, and companions who modeled emotional clarity without hardness,

and positivity without denial - you revealed that the deepest form of intelligence begins with the emotional ground we choose to stand on.

Book Overview: What is this book about?

Positivity: Pathway to Emotional Intelligence is a reflective, psychologically grounded exploration of why emotional intelligence often fails under real-world pressure—and what allows it to function consistently across stress, uncertainty, and complexity.

Rather than treating emotional intelligence as a collection of skills to be learned or behaviors to be managed, this book reveals a deeper truth: emotional intelligence depends on the **emotional orientation** from which life is met. That orientation is positivity.

In this book, positivity is not presented as optimism, cheerfulness, or motivational thinking. It is defined as an **inner stance of openness, constructiveness, and alignment**—a way of engaging with experience that keeps awareness, regulation, empathy, and judgment available even when circumstances are difficult.

The book begins by examining the emotional climate of modern life. Constant pressure, speed, comparison, and emotional overload have quietly normalized negativity—not as pessimism, but as contraction. Many people live in a state of chronic vigilance and fatigue, which narrows perception and erodes emotional capacity. In such conditions, even intelligent, well-intentioned individuals struggle to access their best judgment, sustain empathy, or respond thoughtfully.

From there, the book reframes positivity as a **pathway** rather than a mood or personality trait. It explains how emotional states expand or constrict perception, how the nervous system shapes response, and why intelligence collapses when emotional energy is depleted. Positivity emerges as the inner condition that keeps intelligence usable.

The middle sections show how positivity supports the core elements of emotional intelligence:

- Self-awareness without self-judgment
- Regulation without suppression or control
- Motivation without pressure or fear
- Empathy without emotional exhaustion
- Social intelligence is rooted in emotional tone rather than technique

Rather than offering quick fixes, the book introduces practical, realistic ways to recalibrate emotional orientation—daily resets, recovery practices, and subtle shifts in awareness that restore inner capacity over time.

The final sections extend the pathway into leadership, relationships, and life transitions. Positivity is not a personal preference but a stabilizing force that supports clarity, trust, resilience, and ethical action in environments of responsibility and uncertainty.

Ultimately, **Positivity: Pathway to Emotional Intelligence** is about choice—not choice as willpower, but as orientation. It invites readers to recognize that the emotional ground they stand on shapes how they perceive, decide, connect, and lead.

Positivity is not the reward at the end of emotional growth.

It is the pathway through which emotional intelligence becomes possible in the first place.

Introduction:
The Missing Pathway Beneath Emotional Intelligence

Why skills alone fail—and why positivity determines whether intelligence can function

Emotional intelligence is widely recognized as essential—for leadership, relationships, learning, and personal well-being. It is taught through frameworks and competencies: self-awareness, emotional regulation, empathy, communication, and decision-making. These skills are practical, observable, and widely endorsed.

Yet for many people, they remain unreliable.

We may understand what emotional intelligence looks like, and even value it deeply, but find ourselves unable to access it when it matters most. Under pressure, we react rather than respond. In emotionally charged moments, awareness collapses into defensiveness or self-criticism. In uncertainty, clarity gives way to urgency or avoidance. The gap between knowing and doing is not a lack of insight—it is a breakdown in the conditions that allow intelligence to operate.

This book begins with a simple but often overlooked truth:

Emotional intelligence does not function in isolation.

It depends on the emotional ground from which we meet experience.

That ground is positivity.

Positivity, as used in this book, has nothing to do with forced optimism, positive thinking, or denying difficulty. It refers to an **inner emotional orientation**—a stance of openness, constructiveness, and alignment that keeps perception, judgment, and response available even under stress.

When positivity is present, awareness widens. Emotions can be felt without overwhelm. Empathy flows without depletion. Choices emerge where reactions once dominated. Emotional intelligence becomes usable.

When positivity is absent, the opposite occurs. Awareness narrows. Emotions become threatening or overwhelming. Regulation turns into suppression. Empathy becomes effortful or draining. Intelligence does not disappear; it simply loses its pathway.

Much of what we label as emotional "failure" is actually a collapse of positivity.

Chronic stress, emotional fatigue, unresolved threat, and constant vigilance gradually erode the inner orientation that intelligence requires. Over time, negativity becomes the default—not as pessimism or complaint, but as contraction. The nervous system prioritizes protection over perception. Survival replaces understanding. Reaction replaces response.

In such a state, no amount of skill training can compensate for the loss of emotional capacity. Techniques may work briefly, but they cannot override a contracted inner stance for long. Skills require a supportive emotional environment to function—

just as reasoning requires oxygen and movement requires space.

This is why positivity is not the outcome of emotional intelligence.

It is the pathway through which emotional intelligence becomes possible.

The chapters that follow explore this pathway from multiple angles. They examine how modern life shapes emotional orientation, why negativity becomes normalized, and how emotional fatigue undermines intelligence. They clarify what positivity truly is, how the nervous system supports it, and why it collapses under pressure.

From there, the book shows how positivity enables the core capacities of emotional intelligence—self-awareness without self-judgment, regulation without resistance, motivation without pressure, empathy without exhaustion, and social intelligence grounded in emotional tone rather than technique.

Rather than offering quick fixes or motivational solutions, this book invites a deeper shift: from managing emotions to cultivating the emotional conditions that allow intelligence to emerge naturally.

Positivity is not something we force.

It is something we restore.

When we understand the emotional ground we stand on, we regain choice—choice in how we perceive, how we respond, and how we live. Emotional intelligence, then, is no longer a fragile ideal, but a stable expression of a positive inner orientation.

This is the pathway this book explores.

Chapter 1 — The Emotional Climate We Live In

How pressure, speed, and comparison shape inner experience

We live inside an emotional climate long before we notice individual emotions.

Just as weather shapes how we dress, move, and plan our day, the emotional atmosphere of modern life quietly shapes how we think, react, and relate. It influences our nervous systems before it reaches our awareness. And unlike the weather, this climate rarely pauses. It follows us into our homes, our relationships, and even our moments of rest.

This book begins here—not with techniques, affirmations, or strategies—but with the environment that determines whether any emotional skill can function at all.

An Invisible Atmosphere of Pressure

Modern life is saturated with pressure. Not always dramatic or overt, but constant and ambient.

Pressure to respond quickly.

Pressure to perform consistently.

Pressure to stay relevant, productive, informed, and available.

Much of this pressure does not come from explicit demands but from a background sense that falling behind is dangerous.

Notifications accumulate. Expectations multiply. Silence feels suspicious. Rest feels earned rather than essential.

Over time, the nervous system adapts—not by becoming calmer, but by becoming vigilant.

This vigilance is subtle. It shows up as a slight tightening in the chest, a readiness to react, a mind that scans for what might go wrong next. It becomes so familiar that it no longer feels like stress; it feels like normal functioning.

But this "normal" state quietly narrows emotional capacity.

Speed as a Default Setting

Speed is not just a feature of modern life; it is a value.

Fast responses are praised. Quick decisions are rewarded. Slowness is often interpreted as incompetence, hesitation, or lack of ambition. Even self-care is framed as something to optimize and compress.

In this environment, emotional processes that require time—reflection, integration, sensing, meaning-making—are treated as inefficiencies.

The result is not just mental fatigue, but emotional shallowness.

When life moves faster than emotional processing, reactions replace responses. Feelings are managed rather than understood. Inner signals are overridden by external demands. Over time, people become highly functional yet emotionally brittle—capable, but easily overwhelmed.

Speed trains the mind to outrun the body. And when that happens, emotional intelligence has no stable ground on which to operate.

The Quiet Tyranny of Comparison

Comparison has always existed. What is new is its scale and intimacy.

Through screens and social platforms, we are continuously exposed to curated moments of success, happiness, confidence, and certainty—often without context, nuance, or reality.

The mind absorbs these images not as information, but as benchmarks.

Comparison does not usually arrive as envy. It arrives as insufficiency.

I should be further along.

I should be coping better.

Others seem to manage this more easily than I do.

These thoughts subtly erode self-trust. They create an internal pressure to perform emotionally—to appear calm, positive, resilient, or unbothered—even when the inner experience tells a different story.

This emotional self-surveillance fragments attention and drains energy. Instead of meeting life as it is, people begin managing how they appear within it.

When the Nervous System Never Fully Rests

Pressure, speed, and comparison converge in the nervous system.

The body does not distinguish between physical and psychological threats. When demands feel constant and evaluation feels ongoing, the system stays partially activated. Muscles remain tense. Breathing becomes shallow. Attention narrows.

This is not acute stress. It is chronic activation.

In such a state, people may still function well—sometimes exceptionally well—but at a cost. Emotional regulation becomes effortful. Empathy feels draining. Patience shortens. Small disruptions provoke disproportionate reactions.

Over time, the capacity for presence erodes.

This is why many people feel exhausted even when life appears "under control." The system is never permitted to settle fully.

Why This Climate Matters More Than We Admit

Emotional intelligence does not operate in a vacuum. It is not simply a set of skills that can be applied regardless of context.

It depends on the emotional climate in which a person lives.

When the climate is contracted—marked by vigilance, urgency, and comparison—intelligence narrows. Perspective shrinks. Creativity declines. Even well-developed skills fail to activate reliably.

This is not a personal failure. It is a systemic condition.

Understanding this changes the conversation. Instead of asking, *Why can't I stay calm?* The more useful question becomes, *What state am I living in most of the time?*

Because emotional capacity is not only about who you are—it is about the environment your nervous system inhabits.

A Threshold Moment

Recognizing the emotional climate we live in is not meant to create blame or withdrawal. It is meant to create orientation.

You cannot change what you cannot see.

You cannot expand within an environment you assume is neutral.

This chapter marks a threshold. From here on, the book will explore what happens when negativity becomes the default, how emotional fatigue accumulates, and why positivity—properly understood—is not naïve or optional, but foundational.

Before anything can be practiced, the ground must be understood.

And before emotional intelligence can be developed, the emotional climate must be acknowledged.

Only then can something different begin.

Chapter 2 — When Negativity Becomes the Default

Understanding emotional contraction and the cost of constant vigilance

Negativity rarely announces itself.

It does not always arrive as pessimism, anger, or despair. More often, it arrives quietly—as caution, control, skepticism, and emotional bracing. It presents itself as realism. As preparedness. As maturity.

And because it feels responsible, it often goes unquestioned.

This chapter is not about labeling people as negative. It is about understanding how negativity becomes a default *state*—a baseline orientation from which life is met—without conscious choice or intention.

Negativity as a Protective Strategy

At its core, negativity is not a flaw. It is a survival strategy.

The human nervous system evolved to prioritize threat detection. Paying attention to what might go wrong kept our ancestors alive. Risk awareness, caution, and vigilance were adaptive responses in uncertain environments.

The problem is not negativity itself.

The problem is when protection becomes permanent.

In modern life, threats are rarely immediate or physical, yet the system treats uncertainty, evaluation, time pressure, and social judgment as ongoing danger signals. The result is a posture of emotional contraction—subtle, chronic, and normalized.

In this posture:

- Attention scans for problems rather than possibilities
- Emotional energy is conserved rather than expressed
- Trust is replaced by control
- Openness feels unsafe

What once protected now constrains.

From Occasional Negativity to Default Orientation

Negativity becomes the default not through dramatic trauma, but through repetition.

Small disappointments.

Unresolved stress.

Unmet expectations.

Moments where openness led to overwhelm or hurt.

Each time the system learns, *Better to be guarded.*

Over time, this learning consolidates into an emotional orientation.

Life is approached with anticipation of difficulty rather than curiosity. Neutral events are interpreted cautiously. Ambiguity is treated as risk.

This orientation often feels intelligent.

After all, expecting problems can look like wisdom. Being prepared can look like strength. Emotional restraint can look like discipline.

But beneath this competence lies contraction.

The Cost of Constant Vigilance

Vigilance consumes energy.

When the nervous system is always scanning, it cannot rest. When it cannot rest, emotional resources diminish. Regulation becomes effortful. Empathy feels costly. Joy feels irresponsible or fleeting.

People living in this state often describe themselves as:

- "Just being realistic."
- "Not getting my hopes up."
- "Staying grounded."
- "Managing expectations."

Yet their inner experience is marked by tension rather than grounding, control rather than clarity.

This is the hidden cost of negativity as a default: it reduces emotional bandwidth.

And when emotional bandwidth is reduced, intelligence narrows.

How Negativity Shapes Perception

Negativity does not just affect mood. It shapes perception.

In a contracted state:

- The mind prioritizes certainty over understanding
- The body tightens, limiting sensory feedback
- Emotional nuance is flattened into right/wrong, safe/unsafe
- Complexity feels overwhelming rather than interesting

This is why people can be highly capable in stable conditions yet struggle under pressure. Their intelligence has not disappeared—it has become inaccessible.

Negativity narrows the field of awareness.

And what we cannot perceive, we cannot respond to skillfully.

Why Positivity Is Often Misunderstood

When negativity dominates, positivity is often misunderstood as denial.

From a contracted state, openness looks naïve. Calm looks passive. Hope looks irresponsible. Positivity is dismissed as motivational language rather than a physiological and emotional condition.

But this misunderstanding arises because positivity is evaluated from within contraction.

From that place, expansion feels unsafe.

This is why many people reject positivity even as they long for relief.

They equate openness with vulnerability and vulnerability with danger—because their system has learned that vigilance is required to cope.

Negativity and the Illusion of Control

One of negativity's most seductive promises is control.

If I anticipate problems, I won't be surprised.

If I stay guarded, I won't be hurt.

If I manage expectations, I won't be disappointed.

Yet this control is often illusory.

While vigilance may reduce surprise, it also reduces aliveness. It limits the connection. It blocks learning. It replaces engagement with management.

Life becomes something to endure rather than participate in.

The Quiet Normalization of Contraction

Perhaps the most dangerous aspect of default negativity is that it feels normal.

Entire cultures operate in this mode. Organizations reward it. Educational systems reinforce it. The media amplifies it. Even personal growth conversations often focus on fixing, correcting, and optimizing rather than expanding.

When everyone is contracted, contraction becomes invisible.

And when contraction is invisible, people blame themselves for the symptoms:

- "Why am I so tired?"
- "Why do I overreact?"
- "Why can't I stay calm?"

The answer is not a lack of discipline or skill.

It is the state in which life is being lived.

A Subtle but Crucial Distinction

Negativity is not the presence of difficult emotions.

It is the *orientation* toward experience.

You can feel sadness without being negative.

You can face challenges without contracting.

You can acknowledge risk without living in vigilance.

What matters is whether the system remains open or closes around the experience.

This distinction will become central as the book unfolds.

What This Chapter Makes Possible

Seeing negativity as a default state—not a personality flaw—creates choice.

It opens the door to compassion rather than self-criticism.

It shifts the focus from fixing emotions to understanding conditions.

It prepares the ground for an altogether different orientation.

The next chapter will explore what happens when this contracted state is sustained over time—how emotional fatigue accumulates, and why even intelligent, capable people begin to lose access to their best thinking.

Because before positivity can be reclaimed, the cost of constant vigilance must be fully understood.

Chapter 3 — The Hidden Price of Emotional Fatigue

Why intelligence fails when emotional energy is depleted Emotional fatigue does not announce itself as collapse.

It arrives quietly—through shortened patience, reduced curiosity, brittle calm, and a growing sense that everything requires more effort than it should. People often describe it as being "fine, just tired," unaware that what is depleted is not motivation or willpower, but emotional energy.

This chapter explores the unseen cost of living in sustained contraction—and why, when emotional energy runs low, intelligence becomes unreliable.

Emotional Energy: The Overlooked Resource

We speak easily about time, attention, and physical energy. Emotional energy, by contrast, is rarely named—yet it underlies all three.

Emotional energy is what allows:

- Regulation without suppression
- Attention without strain
- Empathy without exhaustion
- Choice without delay

It is the capacity that makes emotional intelligence usable rather than theoretical.

When emotional energy is available, people can pause, reflect, and respond.

When it is depleted, reactions replace responses—not because of poor character, but because the system no longer has the capacity to hold complexity.

How Fatigue Accumulates Without Notice

Emotional fatigue is cumulative.

It builds not from single events, but from sustained exposure to:

- Pressure without recovery
- Responsibility without support
- Vigilance without safety
- Interaction without presence

Each moment of self-control, emotional management, and internal bracing draws from the same limited reserve. When that reserve is not replenished, the system adapts by narrowing.

This narrowing is subtle at first. People become efficient, task-focused, emotionally economical.

They stop feeling deeply—not because they do not care, but because caring has become expensive.

Why Intelligence Becomes Inaccessible

Under emotional fatigue, intelligence does not disappear—it becomes inaccessible.

The brain prioritizes survival over insight. Attention shifts toward immediate demands. Long-term thinking, nuance, and perspective recede. Creativity declines. Memory becomes selective. Decision-making becomes rigid or impulsive.

This is why capable people make uncharacteristically poor choices when exhausted. This is why leaders under chronic stress lose empathy. This is why conflicts escalate faster when emotional reserves are low.

Fatigue collapses the space between stimulus and response.

And without space, intelligence cannot operate.

The Myth of Pushing Through

Modern culture often celebrates endurance.

"Push through."

"Power on."

"Stay strong."

While short bursts of effort are sometimes necessary, sustained pushing exacts a hidden cost. The system can perform under strain, but it cannot *recover* under strain.

Pushing through fatigue teaches the nervous system that rest is unsafe or undeserved. Over time, this erodes trust in one's own internal signals. People stop listening to the body's cues—not because they are weak, but because responsiveness feels incompatible with performance.

This disconnect accelerates depletion.

Emotional Fatigue and False Calm

One of the most misunderstood signs of emotional fatigue is calmness.

Not all calm is regulation.

Under depletion, people often display a flat, detached calm—emotionally muted, efficient, and distant. This is not stability; it is conservation. The system has reduced emotional range to preserve energy.

While this state may look composed, it limits connection, creativity, and adaptability. It also makes genuine positivity feel unreachable or artificial.

True calm is expansive. Fatigued calm is narrow.

Why Positivity Feels Impossible When Energy Is Low

When emotional energy is depleted, positivity feels unrealistic.

This is not because positivity is false, but because it requires energy to access openness, curiosity, and trust. Expansion cannot occur when the system is exhausted.

This is why advice to "stay positive" often backfires. It asks for an output that the system cannot produce. The result is frustration, self-criticism, or emotional withdrawal.

Positivity is not a mindset imposed on fatigue.

It is a state that emerges when energy is restored.

The Compounding Effect

Emotional fatigue is self-reinforcing.

As energy drops:

- Regulation becomes harder
- Mistakes increase
- Reactions intensify
- Relationships strain

These consequences create additional stress, further draining reserves. Without interruption, the system enters a loop of depletion and contraction.

This is not burnout yet. It is the pathway toward it.

A Crucial Reframe

Emotional fatigue is not a failure of resilience.

It is evidence of sustained adaptation without recovery.

Understanding this reframes the solution. The answer is not greater discipline or better techniques, but a shift in emotional orientation—one that allows expansion, restoration, and access to intelligence again.

This is where positivity enters the conversation—not as optimism or motivation, but as a foundational condition that replenishes emotional energy rather than consuming it.

Preparing for What Comes Next

This chapter completes the diagnostic arc of the book's first section.

We have seen:

- The emotional climate that shapes inner life
- How negativity becomes a default orientation
- The hidden cost of sustained contraction

The next chapter will challenge one of the most persistent misunderstandings in personal development: what positivity actually is—and why mistaking it for optimism or denial has prevented it from being taken seriously.

Only when positivity is understood correctly can it function as the pathway it truly is.

Chapter 4 — Positivity Is Not What You Think

Separating positivity from optimism, denial, and motivation Positivity has a public relations problem.

For many people, the word evokes forced smiles, motivational slogans, or a refusal to acknowledge difficulty. It is associated with denial, superficial encouragement, or an insistence on "good vibes only." Serious thinkers often reject it as naïve. Those under pressure experience it as unrealistic.

And yet, what this book calls *positivity* has nothing to do with pretending things are fine.

This chapter clears the conceptual ground. It separates positivity from the versions that have made it untrustworthy—and reveals why misunderstanding positivity has quietly limited emotional intelligence itself.

Why Positivity Was Reduced to Optimism

Optimism is a belief about outcomes.

It answers questions like:

- Will this work out?
- Will things improve?
- Is the future favorable?

Positivity, as it is commonly framed, has been collapsed into this belief system. To "be positive" is to expect good results or to focus on bright possibilities.

But optimism is cognitive. It lives in thought.

Positivity, as an emotional foundation, lives in the nervous system.

When positivity is mistaken for optimism, it becomes fragile. If circumstances deteriorate, optimism collapses—and positivity collapses with it.

This is why many people abandon positivity during hardship, assuming it has nothing to offer when life is uncertain or painful.

In reality, positivity does not require positive outcomes.

Positivity Is Not Denial

Denial avoids discomfort by refusing to acknowledge reality.

True positivity does the opposite. It increases the capacity to stay present with difficulty without closing down.

Denial says, This isn't happening.

Positivity says, This is happening—and I can remain open while facing it.

The difference is subtle but profound.

Denial numbs. Positivity stabilizes.

Denial bypasses emotion. Positivity allows emotion to move without overwhelming the system.

When positivity is confused with denial, people learn to distrust it.

They associate it with emotional suppression rather than resilience.

Positivity Is Not Motivation

Motivation is effort-based. It relies on pushing, striving, and self-coercion.

"Think positive" is often used as a motivational command—an attempt to override fatigue, doubt, or fear with mental force. This version of positivity is exhausting, especially for people already depleted.

Positivity, as this book defines it, does not demand effort.

It changes the *state* from which effort arises.

In a positive state, action flows more easily. Focus widens. Regulation stabilizes.

Energy becomes available rather than consumed.

This is why positivity cannot be willed into existence when emotional reserves are low.

It is not a command; it is a condition.

What Positivity Actually Is

Positivity is an emotional orientation of openness and expansion.

It is the state in which:

- The nervous system feels sufficiently safe to explore
- Attention widens rather than narrows
- Experience is met with curiosity rather than defense
- Possibility is not forced, but allowed

Positivity does not mean feeling good. It means being *open*.

You can be in grief and still be positive.

You can face conflict and still be positive.

You can acknowledge risk and still be positive.

Because positivity is not about content—it is about capacity.

Expansion Versus Contraction

Throughout this book, two orientations will recur: contraction and expansion.

- **Contraction** narrows perception, increases vigilance, and conserves energy
- **Expansion** widens perception, restores access to intelligence, and replenishes energy

Negativity is not the presence of difficulty—it is contraction in response to difficulty.

Positivity is not the absence of difficulty—it is expansion in its presence.

This distinction reframes emotional maturity. Strength is no longer measured by toughness or suppression, but by the ability to remain open without being overwhelmed.

Why Positivity Has Been Undervalued

Because positivity was framed as belief, denial, or motivation, it was excluded from serious discussions of intelligence and leadership.

Skills were taught instead. Techniques were emphasized. Frameworks proliferated.

But without a positive emotional orientation, these tools operate inconsistently. They work in calm conditions and fail under pressure. They sound good in theory and disappear in practice.

Positivity was dismissed not because it lacked value—but because it was misunderstood.

The Science Beneath the Misconception

When the system is in a positive state, the brain operates differently.

Perception widens. Cognitive flexibility increases. Pattern recognition improves. Social understanding deepens. Learning accelerates.

This is not philosophy. It is physiology.

Positivity shifts the nervous system from threat-dominant functioning toward exploration and integration. Intelligence becomes accessible again—not because problems vanish, but because capacity returns.

Why This Redefinition Matters

If positivity is misunderstood, it will never be cultivated deliberately.

People will continue to chase techniques while ignoring the state that determines whether those techniques can be used. They will blame themselves for failing to "apply" emotional intelligence, unaware that the conditions for application are missing.

This chapter reclaims positivity as foundational—not optional, not naïve, not cosmetic.

What Comes Next

With this reframing in place, the book now turns toward understanding positivity more deeply—not as a concept, but as an orientation that can be recognized, stabilized, and strengthened.

The next chapter explores positivity as an emotional orientation—how it shapes perception, behavior, and decision-making long before conscious choice enters the picture.

Because once positivity is understood correctly, it becomes clear why it is not the opposite of realism—but the condition that makes realism usable.

Chapter 5 — Positivity as Emotional Orientation

The inner posture from which reality is met Positivity is not something you add to experience.

It is the *posture* from which experience is met.

This distinction changes everything.

When positivity is treated as an attitude or technique, it becomes fragile and optional. When it is understood as an emotional orientation, it becomes foundational—shaping perception, meaning, and response before conscious thought intervenes.

This chapter explores positivity not as a feeling, but as the inner stance that determines how reality is received.

Orientation Comes Before Interpretation

Before the mind interprets an event, the body has already oriented toward it.

This orientation happens beneath awareness. It is expressed in muscle tone, breathing patterns, attentional focus, and emotional readiness. It answers a single, unconscious question:

Is this safe enough to engage with?

A contracted orientation meets life defensively.

An expanded orientation meets life receptively.

Positivity lives here—not in the story we tell ourselves, but in the stance the system adopts before the story begins.

The Difference Between Emotion and Orientation

Emotions are transient. They rise and fall in response to events.

Orientation is enduring. It shapes how emotions are processed.

Two people can feel the same emotion—fear, sadness, uncertainty—while holding very different orientations toward it. One contracts and braces. The other stays open and present.

The emotion is the same. The experience is not.

Positivity, as an orientation, allows emotions to move through the system without closing it down. Negativity, as an orientation, restricts movement and narrows response.

How Positivity Expands Perception

In a positive orientation:

- Attention widens
- Sensory input increases
- Context becomes visible
- Nuance returns

The mind is no longer fixated on control or defense. It can notice subtleties, patterns, and relational cues that are invisible in contraction.

This is why positivity supports intelligence. It restores access to information.

When the system is open, perception becomes richer. And richer perception leads to wiser response.

Positivity and Emotional Safety

Positivity does not mean the absence of threat. It means the *presence of sufficient safety.*

Safety here is not situational—it is internal.

A positive orientation signals to the nervous system: *I can stay here.*

This signal enables natural regulation. Breathing deepens. Muscles soften. Emotional range expands.

From this state, difficulty can be faced without escalation.

This is why positivity is not avoidance—it is the condition that makes engagement possible.

Why Orientation Determines Choice

Choice requires space.

When orientation is contracted, the space between stimulus and response collapses. Reactions dominate. Behavior becomes predictable and rigid.

When orientation is positive, space reappears. This space allows:

- Pause
- Perspective
- Deliberate response

Emotional intelligence is not the presence of better options—it is the ability to *see* them.

Positivity restores that visibility.

The Self-Reinforcing Nature of Orientation

Orientation shapes experience, and experience reinforces orientation.

In contraction, the world appears hostile or demanding. This perception justifies further vigilance.

In expansion, the world appears workable or meaningful. This perception supports openness.

Neither orientation is a lie. Each selectively filters reality.

Understanding this reveals why positivity must be cultivated intentionally.

Without awareness, the system defaults to contraction—especially under pressure.

Positivity Without Performance

One of the most important clarifications is this: positivity does not require emotional performance.

You do not need to appear upbeat.

You do not need to suppress doubt.

You do not need to generate enthusiasm.

A positive orientation can be quiet, grounded, and serious.

It is felt not as excitement, but as *availability*.

Orientation Is Trainable

Because orientation is embodied, it can be influenced.

Small shifts in attention, breathing, posture, and awareness can move the system from contraction toward expansion. These shifts are not dramatic, but cumulative.

Over time, positivity becomes less of an effort and more of a baseline.

This is not a personality change. It is a regulation of the state.

Why This Chapter Matters

Understanding positivity as emotional orientation resolves a central puzzle: why people can understand emotional intelligence intellectually yet fail to live it consistently.

The missing link is not knowledge.

It is orientation.

Without a positive orientation, skills remain theoretical. With it, intelligence becomes accessible in real time.

Looking Ahead

The next chapter will explore how this orientation is reflected in the brain—how expansion and threat shape perception, decision-making, and emotional regulation at a neurological level.

Because positivity is not abstract, it is embodied, measurable, and deeply human.

And once its mechanics are understood, its power becomes undeniable.

Chapter 6 — The Brain Under Expansion and Threat

How emotional states widen or narrow perception. The brain does not simply process reality.

It *filters* it.

What you notice, how you interpret events, and what options you perceive are shaped less by intelligence than by emotional state.

Long before conscious reasoning begins, the brain has already decided what kind of world you are in—and how much of it you are allowed to see.

This chapter explores what happens inside the brain under two dominant conditions: expansion and threat. Understanding this distinction reveals why emotional intelligence flourishes in some moments and disappears in others.

Two Modes, One Brain

The brain operates in different functional modes depending on perceived safety.

When the system senses threat—whether physical, social, or psychological—it shifts into a protective configuration. Resources are redirected toward survival.

Speed and certainty are prioritized over nuance and integration.

When the system senses sufficient safety, the brain shifts into an expansive configuration.

Exploration, learning, connection, and creativity become possible.

These are not philosophical states. They are biological realities.

The Brain Under Threat

Under threat, the brain narrows.

Attention becomes selective, scanning for danger or error. Peripheral awareness diminishes.

Ambiguity feels intolerable. The nervous system prepares for action rather than understanding.

In this state:

- Thinking becomes binary
- Memory retrieval favors past threats
- Emotional regulation requires effort
- Empathy declines
- Creativity shuts down

This is why people under pressure often feel "less intelligent." They are not losing capability; they are operating in a restricted mode.

Threat prioritizes survival over insight.

Why Threat Is So Easily Activated

The modern brain treats many everyday experiences as threats:

- Being evaluated
- Being rushed
- Being compared
- Being uncertain
- Being emotionally exposed

These experiences do not endanger survival, yet they activate the same neural circuits as physical danger. The brain is conservative by design. It would rather overreact than miss a risk.

As a result, many people spend much of their lives in low-grade threat—functional, capable, but narrowed.

The Brain Under Expansion

When the system shifts out of threat, the brain widens.

Attention becomes flexible. Multiple perspectives can be held simultaneously. Emotional signals are processed rather than suppressed. Learning accelerates.

In this state:

- Perception is richer
- Decision-making is more adaptive
- Emotional regulation is easier
- Empathy becomes natural
- Meaning emerges

Expansion does not require pleasure or ease. It requires *safety*.

This is why positivity—understood as an emotional orientation—creates access to intelligence. It signals the brain that exploration is possible.

Expansion and the Prefrontal Cortex

In expansive states, higher-order brain functions become accessible.

Reflection, planning, ethical reasoning, and self-awareness rely on neural integration.

These capacities are compromised under threat and restored under expansion.

This explains a common experience: people often know what to do, but cannot do it when stressed. The knowledge is intact; access is blocked.

Expansion restores access.

Why Willpower Fails Under Threat

Willpower depends on cognitive resources.

Under threat, those resources are redirected. Trying to "force" calm or rationality in a threatened brain is like asking a fire alarm to analyze poetry.

This is why emotional intelligence cannot be applied through effort alone. The brain must be in a state that allows it.

Positivity does not override threat. It *resolves* it by shifting orientation.

The Feedback Loop Between State and Perception

Brain state shapes perception, and perception reinforces brain state.

In threat:

- The world appears hostile or overwhelming
- This perception justifies vigilance
- Vigilance maintains the threat

In expansion:

- The world appears navigable
- This perception supports openness
- Openness sustains expansion

Neither loop is chosen consciously. Both feel self-evident.

Recognizing this loop is liberating. It shows that perception is not always truth—it is state-dependent.

Why Intelligence Needs Expansion

Intelligence requires integration.

It requires access to memory, emotion, context, values, and long-term perspective.

These capacities depend on neural cooperation—not dominance by survival circuits.

Expansion allows this cooperation. Threat fragments it.

This is why the most intelligent responses often emerge after calming down—not because the problem changed, but because the brain did.

A Subtle but Powerful Shift

The goal is not to eliminate the threat. That is neither possible nor desirable.

The goal is to recognize when the brain has narrowed—and to restore expansion before demanding intelligence.

This shift changes how we relate to ourselves. Instead of asking, *Why am I failing?*

We begin by asking, "What state am I in?"

That question alone creates space.

What Comes Next

Understanding the brain under expansion and threat prepares us for the next step: interruption.

If negativity loops and threat states arise automatically, how can they be interrupted without suppression or force?

The next chapter explores how reactive cycles form—and how they can be gently, reliably broken.

Because once expansion is restored, intelligence does not need to be taught.

It reappears.

Chapter 7 — Interrupting the Negativity Loop

Breaking reactive cycles without suppression

Negativity does not persist because people choose it.

It persists because it loops.

Once a contraction becomes familiar, the nervous system begins to recreate it automatically. Perception narrows, reactions intensify, and each reaction reinforces the sense that vigilance is necessary. What begins as a protective response becomes a self-sustaining cycle.

This chapter explores how negativity loops form—and, more importantly, how they can be interrupted without force, denial, or suppression.

What a Negativity Loop Really Is

A negativity loop is not just a thought pattern. It is a whole-system reaction.

It begins with a trigger—often small and ambiguous. The system interprets it as a risk. Attention narrows. The body tightens. Emotion contracts. Behavior becomes reactive.

That behavior then creates consequences: misunderstanding, tension, mistakes, and withdrawal. These consequences confirm the system's original assumption: *I need to stay guarded.*

The loop closes—and prepares to repeat.

Because this process happens beneath conscious awareness, people often believe that circumstances cause their reactions. In reality, circumstances activate a pre-existing orientation.

Why Suppression Makes the Loop Stronger

Most attempts to interrupt negativity rely on suppression.

"Don't think that way."

"Stay calm."

"Be positive."

Suppression addresses the surface but ignores the state beneath it. The nervous system remains activated, even if behavior is controlled.

Energy is consumed maintaining composure, and the loop continues internally.

Suppression teaches the system that its signals are unacceptable.

This increases internal conflict and reinforces vigilance.

True interruption works *with* the system, not against it.

The Small Window That Changes Everything

Every loop contains a small opening.

Between trigger and reaction, there is a moment—often brief, often unnoticed—where orientation can shift.

This moment is not cognitive. It is somatic.

It may appear as:

- A catch in the breath
- A tightening in the jaw
- A rush of urgency
- A narrowing of attention

These signals are not problems. They are invitations.

When they are noticed without judgment, the loop slows.

Interruption Begins With Recognition, Not Correction

The first step in interruption is recognition.

Not analysis. Not fixing.

Simply seeing: *This is a contraction.*

Recognition alone begins to widen perception. It brings the observing system online—restoring a degree of expansion.

This is why naming the state ("I'm tightening," "I'm rushing," "I'm bracing") is more effective than changing the thought.

It shifts orientation from inside the loop to witnessing it from the outside.

Restoring Expansion Through the Body

Because negativity loops are embodied, interruption must include the body.

Simple shifts—slowing the breath, softening the shoulders, widening the visual field—send signals of safety. These signals allow the brain to exit threat mode.

The goal is not relaxation. It is *permission to stay.*

When the system feels safe enough, it stops escalating.

Why Curiosity Breaks the Loop

Curiosity is incompatible with contraction.

When curiosity arises—even briefly—the loop weakens. Attention widens. Judgment softens. New information becomes available.

Curiosity does not mean agreement or positivity. It means openness to what is actually happening.

This is why asking a simple internal question—*What is being protected right now?*—can dissolve reactivity more effectively than trying to override it.

Interrupting Without Self-Blame

One of the most important aspects of interruption is tone.

Negativity loops are strengthened by self-criticism. When people judge themselves for reacting, the system perceives this as an additional threat and tightens further.

Gentle recognition creates safety. Safety restores expansion. Expansion restores intelligence.

This sequence cannot be rushed.

From Loop to Pattern to Choice

With practice, interruption becomes more accessible.

People begin to notice loops earlier—sometimes at the level of sensation rather than emotion. The system learns that contraction does not need to be sustained. Trust in internal regulation grows.

Eventually, what once felt automatic becomes optional.

This is not control. It is capacity.

Why This Is the Turning Point

This chapter marks a shift in the book.

Up to this point, we have explored conditions, orientations, and mechanisms. From here on, the focus turns toward lived application—how positivity becomes embodied, reliable, and integrated into daily life.

Interruption is the bridge.

It transforms positivity from a concept into an experience.

What Comes Next

When the system can interrupt negativity loops, it becomes receptive. Emotional energy begins to return. Presence becomes possible.

The next chapter explores where emotional choice truly begins—before behavior, before words, before strategy.

Because once loops are interrupted, something remarkable happens:

You regain the space to choose.

Chapter 8 — Emotional Choice Begins Here

Where awareness turns into response

Most people believe choice begins with action.

They assume that emotional intelligence is about choosing the right words, the right behavior, or the right decision once a situation has already unfolded. But by the time action is required, the most important choice has often already been made.

Emotional choice begins earlier—at the level of awareness.

This chapter explores where choice actually lives, why it is often unavailable, and how it becomes accessible again once the system is no longer trapped in reactivity.

Why Choice Disappears Under Pressure

Under pressure, people do not lose values or intelligence. They lose *space*.

When the nervous system is activated, perception narrows and time compresses. Everything feels urgent. The body prepares to act, not to reflect. In this state, behavior feels inevitable.

"I had no choice."

"It just happened."

"I reacted before I could think."

These statements are not excuses. They accurately describe a system operating without access to choice.

Choice requires expansion.

The Real Location of Choice

Emotional choice does not occur at the level of behavior.

It occurs at the moment awareness returns.

This moment may be subtle:

- Noticing a tightening before speaking
- Sensing urgency before sending a message
- Feeling withdrawal before disengaging

When awareness enters the experience, even briefly, the loop loosens. Orientation shifts from inside the reaction to observing it.

This is the beginning of choice.

Awareness as a Regulating Force

Awareness is not passive.

When awareness is present, the nervous system receives a signal of coherence. Attention widens. Breathing shifts. The body settles enough for regulation to occur.

This is why awareness alone can change behavior—not through effort, but through state change.

Awareness restores access to options.

Why Emotional Choice Is Not Moral Choice

Emotional choice is often confused with moral discipline.

People believe they *should* choose patience, calm, or kindness. When they fail, they judge themselves.

But emotional choice is not about virtue. It is about capacity.

Without sufficient emotional energy and expansion, the "right" choice is invisible. Demanding better behavior without restoring capacity only increases contraction.

True choice emerges naturally when the system can perceive alternatives.

The Micro-Moment That Matters

Choice lives in micro-moments.

It does not require long reflection or perfect calm. It requires just enough space to notice what is happening before it takes over.

That space might last half a second.

But half a second is enough.

In that moment, the system can:

- Pause instead of reacting

- Breathe instead of pushing
- Listen instead of defending

These are not techniques. They are expressions of regained orientation.

From Automatic to Available

When negativity loops dominate, responses feel automatic.

When loops are interrupted, responses become available.

This shift is subtle but profound.

Life feels less like a series of reactions and more like a sequence of choices—even when outcomes remain uncertain.

People often describe this change as:

- Feeling more grounded
- Feeling less hijacked
- Feeling more themselves

What has returned is not control, but agency.

Choice Without Forcing

The paradox of emotional choice is that it cannot be forced.

Trying to choose calm while contracted only adds effort.

But when awareness is present and expansion restored, calm often arises on its own.

Choice, in this sense, is not selection—it is permission.

Permission for intelligence to operate.

Why This Chapter Is a Pivot

This chapter completes the conceptual arc of the book's first half.

We have moved from:

- Emotional climate
- Default negativity
- Fatigue and contraction
- Redefining positivity
- Understanding orientation
- Seeing the brain under threat
- Interrupting reactive loops

Now we arrive at choice—not as an ideal, but as a lived experience.

From here on, the book turns toward integration.

What Comes Next

The next section explores how this restored capacity expresses itself in daily life—through regulation without suppression, empathy without self-loss, leadership under pressure, and decision-making in uncertainty.

Emotional intelligence will no longer be presented as a skill to master, but as a natural function of presence.

Because when awareness is available, choice follows.

And when choice is available, intelligence has somewhere to live.

Chapter 9 — Self-Awareness Without Self-Judgment

Seeing clearly without criticism

Self-awareness is often described as the cornerstone of emotional intelligence.

Yet for many people, becoming "more aware" only increases self-criticism. They notice their reactions, patterns, and limitations—and then turn that awareness into judgment. What was meant to create freedom becomes another form of pressure.

This chapter reframes self-awareness not as self-monitoring or self-improvement, but as a way of seeing that restores clarity without adding weight.

When Awareness Turns Against Us

Most people were taught awareness as evaluation.

Notice what you did wrong.

Notice what you should have handled better.

Notice where you failed to live up to expectations.

Over time, awareness becomes fused with judgment. The observing mind turns into an internal critic, scanning for flaws rather than understanding.

In this state, awareness does not expand capacity—it tightens it.

People begin to avoid looking inward, not because they lack insight, but because insight has become painful.

The Difference Between Seeing and Assessing

Self-awareness is the ability to *see* experience as it is.

Self-judgment is the impulse to *assess* experience as good or bad, right or wrong, acceptable or unacceptable.

These two often occur so quickly together that they feel inseparable. But they are not the same.

Seeing is neutral.

Assessing is evaluative.

When seeing happens without assessment, something unexpected occurs: the system relaxes.

Why Judgment Feels Necessary

Judgment often masquerades as responsibility.

People believe that if they do not judge themselves, they will not improve. Criticism feels like motivation. Harshness feels like discipline.

But judgment does not create growth—it creates threat.

The nervous system interprets self-criticism as danger. Contraction increases. Learning decreases. Patterns repeat.

What looks like accountability is often self-surveillance.

Awareness as a Safe Witness

Self-awareness becomes transformative when it functions as a safe witness.

A safe witness notices without trying to control. It observes reactions without needing to justify or eliminate them. It allows emotions to be present without amplifying them.

This witnessing stance restores internal safety, and safety is what allows honesty.

Ironically, people become more willing to see their patterns when they stop attacking themselves for having them.

How Judgment Distorts Perception

Judgment narrows perception.

When people judge themselves, they focus on outcomes rather than conditions. They ask, *What's wrong with me?* Instead of *What state was I in?*

This distortion hides important information:

- Fatigue
- Overload

- Fear
- Unmet needs

Without this context, awareness becomes incomplete—and unfair.

Curiosity as the Antidote

Curiosity changes the quality of awareness.

When curiosity replaces judgment, the question shifts:

- From Why am I like this?
- To What is happening here?

Curiosity widens perception. It invites complexity. It allows multiple truths to coexist.

This does not excuse harmful behavior. It explains it. And explanation is what makes change possible.

Self-Awareness and Emotional Choice

Without self-judgment, awareness becomes usable.

Instead of triggering shame or defensiveness, insight creates options.

People can notice the contraction and respond to it. They can sense fatigue and restore energy. They can recognize patterns before they take over.

Awareness becomes the ground of choice rather than a record of failure.

The Paradox of Acceptance

Acceptance is often misunderstood as resignation.

In reality, acceptance is the fastest path to change.

When experience is accepted as it is, energy is no longer spent resisting it.

That energy becomes available for regulation, understanding, and response.

Acceptance does not mean liking what you see. It means allowing it to be seen clearly.

Why This Matters Going Forward

As the book moves into applied presence—regulation, empathy, leadership, decision-making—self-awareness will be essential.

But without this foundation, awareness will sabotage those practices rather than support them.

Self-awareness without self-judgment is not indulgence.

It is precision.

What Comes Next

The next chapter explores regulation without suppression—how emotional stability can be cultivated without numbing, bypassing, or hardening.

Because once awareness is kind, regulation becomes possible.

And when regulation is possible, presence becomes sustainable.

Chapter 10 — Regulation Without Resistance

Stability without emotional shutdown

Most people associate regulation with control.

They imagine holding emotions in check, staying composed, or preventing feelings from showing. Regulation becomes synonymous with restraint—something to be achieved through effort, discipline, or suppression.

But this version of regulation is fragile.

It works until it doesn't. And when it fails, emotions rebound with greater force, leaving people feeling hijacked, ashamed, or exhausted.

This chapter introduces a different understanding: regulation that does not resist emotion, but works *with* it.

Why Resistance Creates Instability

Resistance sends a clear message to the nervous system: *this experience is unsafe*.

When emotions are pushed away, tightened against, or mentally overridden, the system interprets the emotion itself as a threat. Activation increases. Tension rises. The body prepares to defend.

What follows is familiar:

- Emotions intensify rather than settle
- Suppressed feelings resurface later
- Regulation requires constant effort
- Emotional expression becomes unpredictable

Resistance does not calm the system. It provokes it.

What Regulation Actually Is

True regulation is not about stopping emotion.

It is about maintaining internal coherence *while emotion moves*.

In regulated states:

- Emotions are felt without overwhelming the system
- Sensation flows without escalation
- The nervous system remains flexible
- Presence is maintained

Regulation allows feeling without flooding.

This is not emotional numbness. It is emotional *capacity*.

The Role of Safety in Regulation

Regulation depends on safety—not external safety, but internal permission.

When the system senses that emotion is allowed, it stops escalating. Breathing deepens. Muscles soften. The brain exits threat mode.

This is why regulation cannot be forced. Safety cannot be commanded. It must be signaled.

And the most powerful signal is non-resistance.

Letting Emotion Complete Its Cycle

Emotions are biological processes.

They rise, peak, and fall—if they are not interrupted. When allowed to complete their cycle, emotions naturally discharge energy. When blocked, they linger.

Non-resistant regulation allows this cycle to unfold without amplification.

You are not indulging emotion.

You are not analyzing it.

You are not acting it out.

You are staying present while it passes.

Why People Fear Non-Resistance

Many people fear that allowing emotion will lead to loss of control.

They imagine that if they stop resisting, they will be overwhelmed, incapacitated, or consumed.

This fear often comes from past experiences where emotions arose in unsafe conditions—without support, awareness, or grounding.

But non-resistance is not collapse.

It is accompanied by presence.

Presence keeps the system anchored while emotion moves.

Regulation as a Relational Skill

Regulation is often framed as an individual task, but it is deeply relational.

When people feel emotionally met—seen, understood, not judged—their nervous systems regulate more easily.

Internal regulation mirrors external safety.

This is why self-awareness without judgment matters. It creates an internal relationship that supports regulation rather than undermining it.

You become a safe presence to yourself.

From Control to Containment

Control tries to eliminate emotion.

Containment allows emotion without letting it take over.

Containment is spacious. It holds experience gently, without tightening. It provides boundaries without force.

In containment, emotions do not need to shout to be heard.

How Regulation Restores Energy

Resistance is exhausting.

Non-resistant regulation conserves energy.

When the system no longer fights itself, emotional energy is freed. Fatigue eases. Clarity returns. Intelligence becomes accessible again.

This is why regulation without resistance feels stabilizing rather than draining.

Why This Chapter Matters

Without this understanding, regulation practices often become another form of self-control—subtle, sophisticated, but still resistant.

With it, regulation becomes sustainable.

You are no longer managing emotions from above.

You are accompanying them from within.

What Comes Next

With regulation established, the system can remain open in a relationship.

The next chapter explores empathy without self-loss—how to stay connected to others without absorbing, collapsing, or exhausting yourself.

Because presence is not only internal.

It is relational.

And regulation without resistance is what makes that possible.

Chapter 11 — Motivation Without Pressure

Energy that arises from alignment, not force most people believe motivation requires pressure.

Deadlines. Expectations. Consequences. Self-talk that pushes harder when energy fades. Motivation becomes something that must be generated through urgency or fear of falling behind.

This approach can work—for a while.

But over time, pressure-based motivation drains emotional energy, increases resistance, and quietly undermines the very momentum it seeks to create. What looks like drive often masks strain.

This chapter explores a different source of motivation—one that does not rely on pressure, coercion, or self-criticism.

Why Pressure Seems Necessary

Pressure feels effective because it moves.

Under threat, the nervous system mobilizes. Attention sharpens. Action accelerates. Tasks get done. In short bursts, pressure delivers results.

The problem is sustainability.

Pressure activates contraction. Contraction consumes energy. Over time, motivation becomes brittle—dependent on urgency, external validation, or fear of consequences.

When pressure lifts, motivation collapses.

This is why people feel productive but depleted, driven but disconnected.

The Hidden Cost of Pushing

Pressure-based motivation trains the system to associate action with strain.

Work becomes something to endure. Progress becomes something to survive. Rest feels guilty. Stillness feels unsafe.

Eventually, resistance appears—not as laziness, but as exhaustion, procrastination, or emotional withdrawal.

The system is not failing.

It is protecting itself.

What Motivation Really Is

Motivation is not willpower.

It is energy directed toward engagement.

When emotional energy is available and orientation is open, motivation arises naturally. Curiosity pulls attention forward.

Meaning sustains effort. Action feels purposeful rather than forced.

Motivation, at its core, is relational—it reflects how the system relates to what it is being asked to do.

Alignment as a Source of Energy

Motivation strengthens when action aligns with values, meaning, or genuine interest.

This alignment does not need to be dramatic. It may be subtle:

- A sense of relevance
- A feeling of contribution
- A quiet "yes" in the body

When alignment is present, less effort is required. The system does not need to be pushed; it moves on its own.

Pressure compensates for misalignment. Alignment makes pressure unnecessary.

Why Resistance Is Information

When motivation drops, most people respond by pushing harder.

But resistance is not an enemy. It is data.

Resistance often signals:

- Emotional fatigue

- Loss of meaning
- Overextension
- Unacknowledged emotion

Ignoring this information increases depletion. Listening to it restores capacity.

Motivation without pressure begins by respecting resistance rather than fighting it.

From Forcing to Inviting

Pressure commands action.

Invites engagement.

An invitation leaves room for choice. It respects the system's current state. It allows pacing, adjustment, and reorientation.

This does not mean abandoning responsibility. It means approaching responsibility from a place of presence rather than threat.

Paradoxically, when the system feels invited rather than forced, follow-through improves.

Motivation and Emotional Safety

Just as learning and intelligence require safety, so does motivation.

When the system feels emotionally safe, it explores. It initiates. It persists.

When it feels threatened, it complies—or shuts down.

Motivation rooted in safety is quieter but more durable. It does not spike and crash. It hums.

Effort Without Strain

Motivation without pressure does not eliminate effort.

It changes the *quality* of effort.

Effort becomes steady rather than frantic. Focus becomes sustained rather than urgent. Progress feels cumulative rather than exhausting.

This is not complacency. It is efficiency without self-violence.

Why This Chapter Matters

Many people try to build presence, regulation, and emotional intelligence while still motivating themselves through pressure.

This creates internal conflict.

Presence softens. Pressure tightens. The system oscillates.

Understanding motivation without pressure allows all the previous chapters to integrate. Energy begins to flow instead of being extracted.

What Comes Next

With motivation no longer dependent on force, relationships change.

The next chapter explores empathy without self-loss—how to stay open to others without absorbing their emotions or abandoning your own center.

Because sustainable motivation is not just about action.

It is about connection—without depletion.

Chapter 12 — Empathy Without Exhaustion

Staying open without losing yourself empathy is often treated as an emotional obligation.

To be a good person, a good leader, or a good listener, we are expected to feel deeply with others, to absorb their emotions, and to carry their experiences alongside our own. When empathy is framed this way, exhaustion is not a side effect—it is inevitable.

This chapter reframes empathy not as emotional absorption, but as a form of presence that allows connection without depletion.

Why Empathy Becomes Draining

Empathy becomes exhausting when it turns into *merging*.

Instead of witnessing another person's experience, the system absorbs it. Emotional boundaries blur. The nervous system mirrors distress without regulation. Over time, this leads to compassion fatigue, emotional withdrawal, or numbing.

People often respond by hardening—pulling back to protect themselves. But this protection comes at the cost of connection.

The problem is not empathy itself.

It is the absence of regulation and boundaries.

The Difference Between Empathy and Absorption

Empathy is the ability to sense and understand another's emotional experience.

Absorption is the loss of separation between their experience and yours.

In empathy:

- You remain grounded in yourself
- The other person feels seen
- Emotional information flows without overwhelm

In absorption:

- Your system takes on their activation
- Clarity diminishes
- Fatigue accumulates

Empathy without exhaustion depends on maintaining this distinction.

Regulation as the Foundation of Empathy

Regulation makes empathy sustainable.

When the nervous system is regulated, it can remain open without being destabilized. Emotions are felt *with* another person, not *for* them.

This is why self-regulation is not selfish. It is relational.

Without regulation, empathy collapses into either over-identification or withdrawal.

Presence Without Fixing

One of the hidden drains on empathy is the urge to fix.

When someone shares pain, the system often rushes to solve, advise, or relieve discomfort—sometimes to ease the listener's own unease rather than the speaker's need.

Presence does not require fixing.

Often, being emotionally met is more regulating than receiving solutions. When the listener stays present without urgency, both systems settle.

Empathy deepens without effort.

Boundaries as an Expression of Care

Boundaries are often misunderstood as distance.

In reality, boundaries create *containment*.

Clear internal boundaries allow empathy to flow safely. They signal to the nervous system: *I can stay connected without losing myself.*

Boundaries are not walls. They are permeable structures that allow exchange without collapse.

Why Self-Awareness Matters Here

Empathy without exhaustion requires awareness of one's own state.

When fatigue, irritation, or overwhelm are ignored, empathy becomes performative. When they are acknowledged, empathy becomes honest.

Self-awareness allows you to adjust—pausing, grounding, or stepping back when needed—without guilt or withdrawal.

This preserves both connection and capacity.

The Paradox of Spacious Empathy

When empathy is not forced, it expands.

Spacious empathy does not rush. It listens deeply. It allows silence. It respects complexity.

Ironically, this form of empathy often feels more supportive to others than intense emotional involvement. It communicates steadiness rather than alarm.

People feel held, not handled.

Empathy in Leadership and Daily Life

In leadership, empathy without exhaustion allows authority without distance.

In relationships, it allows closeness without entanglement.

In caregiving roles, it prevents burnout.

This form of empathy is not dramatic. It is reliable. And reliability builds trust.

Why This Chapter Matters

Without this distinction, people oscillate between over-giving and shutting down.

With it, empathy becomes sustainable—an expression of presence rather than sacrifice.

Empathy no longer costs energy.

It flows from stability.

What Comes Next

With empathy grounded in regulation and boundaries, the system can engage with uncertainty and complexity.

The next chapter explores decision-making in the face of uncertainty—how clarity emerges not from certainty but from presence.

Because when empathy is stable, perspective widens.

And when perspective widens, wisdom follows.

Chapter 13 — Social Intelligence and Emotional Tone

The atmosphere you create before you speak.

Social intelligence is often taught as a set of skills: reading body language, choosing the right words, and adapting to context. While these skills matter, they are secondary.

Before words are spoken, something else is already communicating.

Tone.

Not vocal tone alone, but emotional tone—the state you bring into an interaction. This tone is felt immediately and unconsciously by others. It shapes trust, openness, and influence long before content is processed.

This chapter explores why emotional tone is the foundation of social intelligence—and how it arises naturally from presence rather than performance.

Why Tone Speaks First

Human nervous systems are exquisitely sensitive to one another.

Before meaning is analyzed, systems scan for safety, intention, and coherence. This happens beneath awareness. People may not know *why* they feel at ease or guarded around someone— but they feel it instantly.

Emotional tone answers unspoken questions:

- Is this person grounded or tense?
- Are they open or defensive?
- Are they present or preoccupied?

Words arrive later.

This is why technically "correct" communication can still fail. The message is overshadowed by the state delivering it.

Tone Is a State, Not a Strategy

Many people try to manage tone deliberately—softening their voice, choosing careful language, smiling at the right moments.

These strategies can help, but they are fragile.

If the underlying state is anxious, rushed, or guarded, the tone will leak through. People sense incongruence. Trust erodes.

Authentic emotional tone cannot be manufactured.

It emerges from regulation and orientation.

How Contraction Shapes Social Interaction

In contraction, social intelligence narrows.

Attention turns inward. The system monitors itself: *Am I saying the right thing? How am I being perceived?* This self-focus reduces availability to others.

Contraction often produces tones such as:

- Urgency
- Defensiveness
- Authority without warmth
- Politeness without presence

These tones are not intentional. They are expressions of a nervous system under strain.

Expansion and Relational Ease

In expansion, social intelligence becomes effortless.

Attention widens outward. Listening deepens. Responses arise naturally. Silence becomes comfortable rather than awkward.

Expanded tone often carries:

- Calm
- Warmth
- Clarity
- Quiet confidence

People feel met rather than managed.

This is why presence is so influential. It changes interactions without requiring technique.

The Contagious Nature of Emotional Tone

Emotional tone is contagious.

A regulated system invites regulation in others. A rushed system spreads urgency. A defensive tone evokes defensiveness.

This contagion is not psychological—it is physiological. Nervous systems synchronize.

This explains why some people stabilize rooms simply by entering them, while others escalate tension without saying much at all.

Social intelligence, in this sense, is environmental.

Tone and Power Dynamics

Tone becomes especially important in positions of authority.

When power is combined with contraction, people feel unsafe—even if intentions are good. Feedback is filtered. Honesty diminishes. Compliance replaces engagement.

When power is combined with presence, people relax. Information flows. Creativity emerges.

Leadership is communicated through tone more than instruction.

Why Listening Is More Than Hearing

Listening is often framed as a behavior: maintain eye contact, nod, paraphrase.

But real listening is a *state*.

When the listener is regulated and present, the speaker feels it. Their nervous system settles. They speak more freely. Meaning deepens.

When the listener is distracted or tense, the speaker contracts—even if the listener appears attentive.

Listening quality reflects inner orientation.

Repairing Social Ruptures Through Tone

Mistakes in communication are inevitable.

What repairs them is not explanation, but tone.

A grounded, open tone signals safety. It allows misunderstanding to soften. It restores the connection faster than justification ever could.

Tone communicates willingness to meet rather than win.

Why This Chapter Matters

Social intelligence is often taught as outward adaptation.

This chapter reveals it as inward regulation.

When emotional tone is stable, skills become secondary. Influence becomes natural. Relationships feel less effortful.

You no longer manage interactions.

You shape the field in which they occur.

What Comes Next

With social intelligence grounded in tone, the book now turns toward situations that test presence most deeply: pressure, conflict, and uncertainty.

The next chapter explores how emotional tone holds—or collapses—under pressure, and how presence can be sustained when stakes are high.

Because social intelligence matters most when it is hardest to maintain.

And that is where presence proves its value.

Chapter 14 — The Daily Reset

Restoring presence in the midst of ordinary life

Presence is not something you achieve once and keep.

It fluctuates. It fades under pressure. It is lost in distraction, urgency, and emotional accumulation. This is not a failure of discipline—it is the reality of living in a demanding world.

What matters is not staying present at all times, but knowing how to *return*.

This chapter introduces the idea of the daily reset: a simple, repeatable way of restoring emotional orientation without effort, force, or withdrawal from life.

Why Presence Drifts

Presence fades quietly.

It drifts as attention fragments as emotions accumulate without processing. The nervous system absorbs pressure without release.

Most people do not notice the moment presence is lost. They notice only the consequences:

- Reactivity
- Fatigue
- Disconnection
- Mental noise

Trying to "do better" from this state only adds pressure.

A reset is required—not improvement.

Reset Is Not Escape

A daily reset is not about retreating from responsibility or stepping away from life.

It is about returning to life.

Reset restores orientation. It brings the system back from contraction to expansion, from reaction to awareness.

This can happen in minutes.

The Three Elements of a Reset

A genuine reset always includes three elements:

1. **Interruption**
2. Pausing the momentum of reactivity—often by stopping, slowing, or shifting attention.
3. **Reorientation**
4. Re-establishing contact with the body, breath, or present-moment sensation.
5. **Permission**
6. Allowing the system to settle without demanding immediate clarity or performance.

None of these requires analysis or motivation. They work because they change state.

Small, Frequent, Unremarkable

Resets do not need to be dramatic.

In fact, their power lies in being small and frequent:

- A few conscious breaths
- A brief pause before responding
- A moment of stillness between tasks

These moments accumulate. They prevent emotional debt from building.

The system learns that restoration is available.

Why Ritual Helps

Ritual creates reliability.

When resets are built into daily rhythms—morning, transitions, evening—the nervous system begins to anticipate safety. This anticipation itself reduces contraction.

Ritual does not need to be spiritual or symbolic. It needs to be consistent.

Consistency builds trust.

Reset Without Self-Improvement

The daily reset is not a self-improvement exercise.

It does not aim to fix mood, eliminate emotion, or optimize performance.

Its purpose is simpler: to restore presence.

From presence, everything else becomes easier.

What Happens Over Time

With regular resets:

- Emotional fatigue decreases
- Reactivity shortens
- Awareness returns faster
- Positivity stabilizes

Presence becomes less fragile—not because life is calmer, but because recovery is practiced.

When Reset Feels Impossible

On difficult days, even pausing can feel like too much.

This is not failure. It is information.

On such days, the reset may be nothing more than noticing that you are contracted—and allowing that to be seen without judgment.

Even that is a return.

Why This Chapter Matters

Many people try to live with presence as a constant state, only to feel discouraged when they fail.

This chapter replaces that expectation with a humane rhythm: drift and return.

Presence is not maintained by perfection.

It is maintained by practice.

What Comes Next

With the daily reset in place, presence becomes part of ordinary life—not an exceptional state reserved for calm moments.

The next chapter explores presence as a way of being—not something you do occasionally, but how you live, relate, and move through the world.

Because when return becomes natural, presence becomes home.

Chapter 15 — Meeting Difficulty Without Collapse

Staying open when life does not cooperate

Difficulty is inevitable.

What determines our experience of it is not whether it appears, but how the system meets it. Some moments tighten us instantly. Others we can stay with—feel fully—without losing our footing.

This chapter is about that difference.

It explores what allows difficulty to be met without collapse, without hardening, and without retreat into control or avoidance. Not because life becomes easier, but because capacity becomes steadier.

Why Difficulty Triggers Collapse

Collapse is not weakness.

It is what happens when the nervous system perceives a threat without sufficient capacity to hold it.

Under difficulty, several things often happen at once:

- Emotional intensity rises
- Meaning feels threatened
- Identity feels implicated
- Time feels compressed

When these converge, the system contracts. Perspective narrows. Regulation becomes effortful. The body prepares to protect itself.

Collapse may look like:

- Emotional shutdown
- Overreaction
- Withdrawal
- Control or rigidity
- Hopelessness

These are not character flaws. They are protective responses to overload.

The Difference Between Difficulty and Threat

One of the most important distinctions in emotional intelligence is this:

Difficulty is not the same as threat.

Difficulty challenges capacity.

The threat endangers safety.

When difficulty is interpreted as a threat, the system collapses. When it is met as just difficulty or a challenge, the system can stay present.

This distinction is not intellectual. It is embodied.

Meeting difficulty without collapse requires the nervous system to feel *safe enough* to remain open.

Stability Does Not Mean Comfort

Meeting difficulty without collapse does not mean feeling calm, confident, or resolved.

It means remaining *available*.

You may still feel fear, sadness, anger, or uncertainty—but these emotions move through a stable container rather than overwhelming it.

Stability is not the absence of discomfort.

It is the presence of capacity.

The Role of Orientation

Orientation determines whether difficulty collapses or strengthens us.

In contraction:

- Difficulty feels personal
- Meaning feels threatened
- The future feels ominous

In expansion:

- Difficulty feels situational
- Meaning remains intact
- The future remains open

Nothing about the situation has changed. The orientation has.

This is why people can face enormous challenges with grace at times—and feel undone by smaller ones at others.

Staying With, Not Getting Through

A common response to difficulty is urgency: *How do I get through this?*

This question assumes the present moment is intolerable.

Presence asks a different question: Can I stay with this, just as it is, without abandoning myself?

Staying with does not mean resigning or approving.

It means remaining in a relationship with experience rather than fleeing it.

Paradoxically, staying with difficulty often allows it to move faster—because resistance is removed.

Meaning as a Stabilizer

Meaning plays a quiet but powerful role in preventing collapse.

When difficulty is connected to something that matters— values, purpose, care—the system can tolerate more intensity without closing.

Meaning does not eliminate pain.

It contextualizes it.

This context allows difficulty to be endured without losing orientation.

Why Collapse Feels Final—but Isn't

Collapse often feels irreversible in the moment.

"This is too much."

"I can't do this."

"There's no way through."

These thoughts arise from a narrowed perception, not objective reality.

When orientation shifts—even slightly—possibility returns. Space reappears.

Intelligence becomes accessible again.

Collapse is a state, not a truth.

Meeting Difficulty as Practice

The capacity to meet difficulty without collapse is built over time.

It grows through:

- Repeated interruption of contraction
- Regulation without resistance
- Self-awareness without judgment

- Daily returns to presence

Each time difficulty is met without abandoning openness, the system learns something new: *I can stay.*

This learning accumulates.

Why This Chapter Matters

Much of emotional intelligence is tested not in calm moments but in adversity.

Without this capacity, all earlier insights remain conditional— available only when life cooperates.

With it, presence becomes resilient.

You are no longer organized around avoiding difficulty.

You are organized around meeting it.

A Quiet Reorientation

Meeting difficulty without collapse does not make you invulnerable.

It makes you *grounded*.

Grounded enough to feel deeply.

Grounded enough to respond wisely.

Grounded enough to remain yourself when conditions are hard.

This is not mastery.

It is maturity.

And it is one of the clearest expressions of true emotional intelligence.

Chapter 16 — Reframing Without Distortion

Seeing differently without lying to yourself

Reframing is often misunderstood as positive thinking.

When people hear "reframe," they imagine forcing a better story onto an unwanted experience—looking for silver linings, minimizing pain, or telling themselves things are fine when they are not.

This kind of reframing feels dishonest. And the nervous system knows it.

This chapter explores a different kind of reframing—one that clarifies rather than distorts, expands rather than overrides, and restores perspective without betraying reality.

Why Reframing Gets a Bad Reputation

Reframing fails when it is used too early.

When the system is still contracted, any attempt to reinterpret experience feels like invalidation. Pain is dismissed. Emotion is bypassed. Resistance increases.

People instinctively reject reframing because they sense the distortion.

You cannot think your way into expansion while the body is still braced.

Reframing Is a Perceptual Shift, Not a Story Change

True reframing does not begin in thought.

It begins in perception.

When orientation shifts from contraction to expansion, perception widens. More information becomes available. Context reappears. Time opens.

Only then does meaning reorganize.

Reframing is not about telling a different story—it is about *seeing* more of the same story.

The Difference Between Distortion and Expansion

Distortion replaces reality.

Expansion includes more of it.

Distortion says:

- "This isn't that bad."
- "Others have it worse."
- "I shouldn't feel this way."

Expansion says:

- "This is painful *and* workable."
- "This matters, *and* it is not the whole story."
- "I can acknowledge this without being defined by it."

The facts remain intact. Perspective changes.

Why Expansion Changes Meaning

Meaning is not fixed.

It emerges from what the system can perceive.

When perception is narrow, meaning collapses into threat, blame, or hopelessness. When perception widens, meaning becomes layered.

This is why reframing feels effortless *after* regulation—but impossible before it.

The mind is not being clever.

It is finally seeing clearly.

Reframing Without Self-Betrayal

One of the deepest harms of forced positivity is self-betrayal.

When people override their own experience, they lose trust in themselves. The system learns that honesty is unsafe.

Reframing without distortion preserves trust.

It allows experience to be fully acknowledged *before* perspective shifts.

Nothing is denied. Nothing is minimized.

The Role of Time in Reframing

Contraction collapses time into urgency.

Expansion restores time.

When time reappears, perspective follows. What felt permanent reveals itself as transient. What felt defining becomes contextual.

Reframing often happens naturally when the system feels it has time to breathe.

Reframing as Integration

True reframing integrates emotion, cognition, and context.

It does not silence emotion.

It does not dominate with logic.

It allows both to inform each other.

The result is not cheerfulness, but coherence.

Why This Chapter Matters

Without this distinction, reframing becomes another tool of pressure—another way to "do it right."

With it, reframing becomes a natural consequence of presence.

You do not need to search for meaning.

Meaning reorganizes itself when perception expands.

What Comes Next

As the book approaches its final chapters, attention turns to integration—how these capacities come together as a way of living rather than a set of practices.

The next chapter explores presence as identity—not something you apply, but something you embody.

Because when reframing is honest, presence becomes stable.

And when presence is stable, life is met as it is—without distortion.

Chapter 17 — Emotional Recovery and Renewal

Restoring capacity after strain

Recovery is rarely taught.

We are taught how to endure, how to cope, how to push through difficulty—but not how to *recover* from it. As a result, many people live in a state of partial depletion, moving from one demand to the next without ever fully restoring emotional capacity.

Renewal becomes an idea rather than an experience.

This chapter explores emotional recovery not as rest alone, but as the restoration of openness, energy, and coherence after strain.

Why Recovery Is Often Missed

Most people confuse recovery with stopping.

They believe that if they pause, take time off, or distract themselves, recovery will occur automatically. Sometimes it does. Often it does not.

Emotional recovery requires more than the absence of demand.

It requires reintegration.

Without integration, strain remains stored in the system. The body may rest, but the nervous system does not reset. Emotional energy remains low even after breaks.

This is why people can feel tired after rest—or anxious during vacations.

Strain That Never Fully Leaves

Emotional strain accumulates quietly.

It comes from:

- Sustained vigilance
- Unresolved emotion
- Incomplete stress cycles
- Constant adaptation without release

When strain is not metabolized, it becomes background tension. People adapt to it. They stop noticing it. But it continues to consume energy.

Recovery begins when this strain is allowed to complete its cycle.

Recovery Is a Process, Not an Event

Recovery is not a single action.

It unfolds through stages:

1. **Safety** — the system senses that it can settle

2. **Discharge** — held activation releases
3. **Integration** — experience reorganizes
4. **Renewal** — energy becomes available again

Skipping stages leads to partial recovery. True renewal requires time, gentleness, and presence.

The Role of Allowing

One of the most powerful elements of recovery is allowing.

Allowing fatigue to be felt without judgment.

Allowing emotion to surface without analysis.

Allowing the system to slow down without guilt.

Allowing is not indulgence.

It is completion.

When experience is allowed, the nervous system no longer has to hold it.

Why Renewal Feels Different From Relief

Relief is the removal of pressure.

Renewal is the return of vitality.

Relief feels like escape.

Renewal feels like *aliveness*.

People often mistake relief for recovery and wonder why energy does not return. Renewal requires more than absence of strain—it requires reconnection to openness, meaning, and embodiment.

Emotional Recovery and Positivity

Positivity plays a critical role in renewal.

Not as cheerfulness, but as expansion.

When the system expands, it begins to trust again. Curiosity returns. Interest reawakens. Emotional range widens.

Renewal is marked not by calm alone, but by renewed engagement with life.

Small Signals of Renewal

Renewal does not announce itself loudly.

It appears subtly:

- A deeper breath
- A spontaneous smile
- A return of humor
- Interest without effort
- Emotional responsiveness

These signals indicate that emotional energy is replenishing.

Why Renewal Cannot Be Forced

Trying to "get back to normal" too quickly interrupts recovery.

Pressure to be productive, positive, or available short-circuits renewal. The system senses expectation and tightens again.

Renewal follows safety, not demand.

Recovery as a Skill

Recovery improves with practice.

When people learn to notice depletion early, allow completion, and restore orientation, renewal becomes more accessible. Emotional setbacks shorten. Fatigue does not linger as long.

Recovery becomes less dramatic and more reliable.

Why This Chapter Matters

Without recovery, presence becomes unsustainable.

Without renewal, emotional intelligence becomes a finite resource rather than a living capacity.

This chapter restores something essential: the permission to recover fully.

A Different Relationship With Effort

Recovery changes how effort is experienced.

Effort no longer drains endlessly.

It is followed by restoration.

Cycles complete.

This rhythm—engagement, strain, recovery, renewal—is natural.

When honored, emotional life regains balance.

Looking Ahead

The final chapters of this book explore how presence, positivity, and emotional intelligence integrate into a way of being—not something managed, but something lived.

Recovery and renewal are not the end of the journey.

They are what make the journey sustainable.

Because only a renewed system can remain open.

And only an open system can live with depth, clarity, and meaning.

Chapter 18 — Positivity in Leadership and Work

Creating environments where intelligence can function

Leadership is often described in terms of strategy, decision-making, and influence.

But beneath every strategy and decision lies something quieter and more powerful: the emotional environment in which people are asked to think, act, and collaborate. This environment determines not only how people feel at work, but also how intelligently they can function.

This chapter explores positivity not as a leadership style, but as an enabling condition—one that allows clarity, responsibility, and creativity to emerge under real-world pressure.

Why Leadership Is an Emotional Act

Every leader shapes emotional climate—whether intentionally or not.

Through tone, pacing, attention, and presence, leaders communicate safety or threat long before they communicate direction. Teams respond accordingly.

In a contracted climate:

- People focus on avoiding mistakes
- Information is filtered
- Initiative declines

- Compliance replaces ownership

In an expanded climate:

- People think more broadly
- Feedback flows upward
- Responsibility is shared
- Learning accelerates

Leadership effectiveness is inseparable from the emotional state it creates.

Positivity as Capacity, Not Cheerfulness

Positivity in leadership is often misunderstood as being upbeat, encouraging, or relentlessly optimistic.

In reality, forced positivity undermines trust.

True positivity is not emotional performance.

It is emotional *capacity*.

A positive leader can:

- Acknowledge difficulty without escalation
- Hold uncertainty without rushing to false certainty
- Address problems without blame
- Stay open under pressure

This kind of positivity feels steady, not enthusiastic. Grounded, not motivational.

The Cost of Threat-Based Work Cultures

Many workplaces operate on a low-grade threat.

Deadlines are framed as emergencies. Mistakes are punished implicitly. Evaluation is constant. Comparison is normalized. Urgency becomes habitual.

While such environments may produce short-term output, they carry hidden costs:

- Reduced innovation
- Emotional fatigue
- Poor decision-making
- Increased turnover
- Erosion of trust

People appear busy, but intelligence is constrained.

Threat narrows thinking. Positivity restores it.

Why Positivity Improves Performance

When people feel safe enough, several things change:

- Attention widens
- Memory improves
- Collaboration deepens
- Initiative increases
- Errors are addressed earlier

These are not cultural niceties. They are functional advantages.

Positivity does not lower standards.

It raises capacity.

People are more accountable—not less—when they are not bracing themselves.

Leading Under Pressure Without Spreading It

Pressure is unavoidable in leadership.

What matters is whether pressure is *absorbed* or *transmitted*.

When leaders are unregulated, pressure spreads. Teams feel rushed, tense, and reactive. When leaders remain grounded, pressure is contained. The system stabilizes.

This is one of the most practical applications of presence:

- Slowing slightly instead of escalating
- Naming reality without alarm
- Creating space before decisions
- Regulating tone before addressing issues

These small actions prevent contraction from cascading through the organization.

Positivity and Psychological Safety

Psychological safety is often discussed as a policy or practice.

In reality, it is felt moment by moment.

People ask silently:

- Can I speak honestly here?
- Will I be punished for mistakes?
- Is uncertainty allowed?

Positivity creates safety by reducing threat—not by removing accountability, but by separating learning from fear.

In psychologically safe environments:

- Problems surface earlier
- Responsibility increases
- Learning becomes continuous

Positivity Is Not Soft Leadership

One of the most persistent myths is that positivity makes leaders less decisive.

The opposite is true.

Leaders operating from expansion:

- See more options
- Integrate more information
- Make clearer decisions
- Adjust faster when conditions change

Decisiveness improves when perception widens.

Positivity does not weaken authority.

It stabilizes it.

Work as an Emotional System

Workplaces are emotional systems, not just operational ones.

Unacknowledged stress circulates. Suppressed frustration leaks. Fatigue shapes behavior. Positivity alters these dynamics by changing orientation at the system level.

When enough individuals operate from expansion, culture shifts—not through slogans, but through lived experience.

Why This Chapter Matters

Many leadership models focus on what leaders should *do*.

This chapter focuses on what leaders must *be*.

Positivity, as an emotional orientation, determines whether intelligence—individual and collective—can function at work.

Without it, even the best strategies underperform.

With it, ordinary people do extraordinary thinking.

A Quiet Responsibility

Leadership carries a quiet responsibility: to shape conditions, not just outcomes.

When leaders understand positivity as capacity rather than optimism, they stop managing emotions and start enabling intelligence.

This is not idealism.

It is realism—at its most practical.

Because in the complexity of modern work, the greatest competitive advantage is not speed or control.

It is the ability to remain open, clear, and human under pressure.

Chapter 19 — Positivity in Relationships

Staying open without losing connection—or yourself

Relationships are where emotional orientation becomes most visible.

At work, roles and structures can mask emotional states. In relationships, they cannot.

How we listen, react, withdraw, or reach out reveals the state from which we are meeting one another.

This chapter explores positivity not as agreement, harmony, or emotional closeness—but as the capacity to remain open, present, and responsive in connection, even when relationships are strained.

Why Relationships Amplify Emotional State

Relationships activate the nervous system more powerfully than most situations.

They touch identity, belonging, history, and unmet needs.

As a result, contraction and expansion are felt more intensely here than anywhere else.

In contraction:

- Small misunderstandings escalate
- The intent is misread

- Defensiveness appears quickly
- Old patterns resurface

In expansion:

- Repair happens faster
- Differences feel workable
- Listening deepens
- Emotional honesty feels safer

The difference is not skill.

It is orientation.

Positivity Is Not Niceness

Positivity in relationships is often confused with being nice, agreeable, or accommodating.

This misunderstanding creates resentment.

True positivity does not avoid conflict.

It allows conflict without collapse.

A positive orientation can say no without attacking, express hurt without blaming, and set boundaries without withdrawing.

Niceness avoids tension.

Positivity holds it.

Emotional Tone Sets the Relationship Field

Just as in leadership, emotional tone shapes relational experience before words are exchanged.

Tone communicates:

- Am I safe to speak?
- Will I be met or defended against?
- Is this interaction open or closed?

When tone is regulated and present, conversations soften—even when content is difficult.

When tone is contracted, even loving words can land harshly.

Why Conflict Becomes Personal

In contraction, conflict feels existential.

The nervous system interprets disagreement as a threat.

The past rushes in.

Meaning collapses into right and wrong, win or lose.

This is why people say things they later regret—not because they mean them, but because perception has narrowed.

Positivity restores context.

It allows disagreement without identity threat.

Staying Open When It's Hardest

The true test of positivity in relationships is not closeness—it is difficulty.

Can you stay present when disappointed?

Can you listen when triggered?

Can you remain curious when hurt?

These capacities do not arise from effort. They arise from regulation.

When the system feels safe enough, openness becomes possible.

Repair as an Expression of Positivity

No relationship avoids rupture.

What matters is repair.

Repair does not require perfect words. It requires tone, presence, and willingness to reconnect.

A regulated, open presence communicates more than explanation ever could: *I am here. I am available.*

This availability restores trust faster than justification.

Boundaries Without Withdrawal

Positivity supports boundaries.

Without expansion, boundaries feel defensive or punitive. With expansion, they feel clear and respectful.

You can say:

- "This doesn't work for me."
- "I need space."
- "I'm not available for this."

without closing your heart or severing the connection.

Boundaries become expressions of care rather than walls.

Why Emotional Availability Matters More Than Agreement

People often believe relationships thrive on agreement.

In reality, they thrive on emotional availability.

When people feel emotionally met, differences are tolerated. When they do not, even agreement feels hollow.

Positivity creates availability—not by smoothing over differences, but by staying present through them.

Relationships as Practice Grounds

Relationships are not obstacles to presence.

They are training grounds.

Each interaction reveals orientation. Each rupture invites awareness. Each repair strengthens capacity.

Positivity in relationships is not about getting it right.

It is about staying engaged.

Why This Chapter Matters

Without positivity, relationships oscillate between closeness and distance, intensity and withdrawal.

With positivity, relationships become more resilient.

- They can stretch without breaking.
- They can hold complexity without collapse.
- They can grow without losing safety.

A Quiet Transformation

When positivity becomes relational, something shifts.

- You stop managing relationships and start *meeting* people.
- You listen more deeply—not to fix, but to understand.
- You speak more honestly—not to win, but to connect.
- You remain yourself—even when emotions run high.

This is not idealism.

It is what becomes possible when emotional orientation is stable.

And it is one of the most meaningful ways positivity expresses itself in a human life.

Chapter 20 — Positivity Through Change and Uncertainty

Staying oriented when the future is unclear

Change and uncertainty unsettle the nervous system more reliably than almost anything else.

They disrupt expectations, threaten identity, and remove familiar reference points. Even positive change can provoke anxiety when outcomes are unknown. In these moments, the system reaches instinctively for control, certainty, or withdrawal.

This chapter explores how positivity—understood as an emotional orientation—helps people navigate change without losing coherence, clarity, or self-trust.

Why Uncertainty Feels Threatening

The human brain is a prediction engine.

It constantly forecasts what will happen next in order to maintain a sense of safety. When the future becomes unclear, prediction fails—and threat circuits activate.

Uncertainty is interpreted as danger, not because it is harmful, but because it is *unknown*.

This is why people often:

- Rush decisions prematurely

- Cling to outdated structures
- Overinterpret information
- Avoid change altogether

These responses are attempts to regain certainty—not wisdom.

The Illusion of Control

In uncertainty, control feels comforting.

Plans multiply. Decisions harden. Rigid positions form. People confuse decisiveness with stability.

But control does not resolve uncertainty—it masks it.

And the cost of this masking is contraction: narrowed perception, reduced flexibility, and increased reactivity.

Positivity offers a different response.

Positivity as Tolerance for Not Knowing

Positivity does not eliminate uncertainty.

It increases tolerance for it.

In a positive orientation, the system can say:

- I don't know yet—and that's okay.
- I can stay present without answers.
- Clarity will emerge in time.

This tolerance prevents premature closure. It keeps perception open.

Uncertainty becomes a space for learning rather than a problem to eliminate.

How Expansion Supports Adaptation

Adaptation requires flexibility.

In expansion:

- Attention remains wide
- Multiple possibilities are considered
- New information is integrated
- Meaning reorganizes organically

This is why people who operate from a positive mindset adapt more effectively to change. They do not panic or freeze. They remain responsive.

Adaptation is not speed.

It is responsiveness over time.

The Emotional Work of Letting Go

Change often requires letting go—of identities, expectations, routines, or narratives.

Letting go is not a cognitive act. It is emotional.

Without regulation and expansion, letting go feels like a loss without ground. With positivity, loss can be held without collapse.

Positivity provides the internal safety needed to release what no longer fits.

Decision-Making Without False Certainty

Uncertainty tempts people into false certainty.

They overcommit to a single option to quiet anxiety. Later, they discover blind spots that were invisible under contraction.

Positivity supports wiser decision-making by allowing provisional decisions.

You can choose a direction while remaining open to adjustment. You can act without pretending the future is settled.

This reduces regret and increases learning.

Why Positivity Prevents Paralysis

At the other extreme, uncertainty can lead to paralysis.

Too many options. Too much risk. Too little clarity.

In contraction, the system waits for certainty that never arrives.

In expansion, movement becomes possible even without complete information.

Positivity does not guarantee outcomes.

It restores the capacity to move.

Change as a Relational Process

Change rarely affects only one person.

Families, teams, and organizations move through uncertainty together. Emotional orientation becomes contagious.

A regulated, open presence stabilizes others. A contracted presence amplifies fear.

Positivity, in this sense, is not private—it is relational.

Why This Chapter Matters

Modern life is defined by uncertainty.

Technological change, social shifts, economic volatility, and personal transitions ensure that clarity is often temporary.

Without a way to meet uncertainty, emotional intelligence remains situational.

With positivity, uncertainty becomes livable.

A Different Relationship With the Future

Positivity through change does not promise optimism.

It offers orientation.

You may not know what is coming.

You may not control outcomes.

You may feel fear, grief, or excitement.

But you remain available.

Available to learn.

Available to respond.

Available to remain yourself.

This is the quiet power of positivity in uncertain times.

Not certainty.

Capacity.

Chapter 21 — A Lifelong Emotional Practice

Living positivity as a way of being

Positivity is not a phase.

It is not a technique you master, a mindset you adopt, or a state you maintain perfectly. It is a practice—one that unfolds over a lifetime, deepening through experience rather than completion.

This final chapter gathers the threads of the book into a single orientation: positivity not as something you *do*, but as something you *live*.

Why There Is No Finish Line

Much of modern self-development is structured around achievement.

Complete the program. Master the skill. Reach the outcome.

But emotional life does not work this way. It moves in cycles. Presence fades and returns.

\Capacity expands and contracts. Understanding deepens through repetition.

Positivity, as described in this book, has no endpoint.

There is only continued engagement.

Practice Without Self-Improvement Pressure

A lifelong emotional practice is not about becoming better.

It is about becoming *more available*.

Available to notice when contraction appears.

Available to return without judgment.

Available to meet life as it is rather than as it should be.

This removes the subtle pressure to perform emotionally.

You are not failing when you lose presence.

You are practicing when you return.

Integration Over Time

What begins as a conscious effort becomes embodied over time.

Interrupting negativity loops becomes quicker.

Regulation becomes less effortful.

Recovery shortens.

Orientation stabilizes.

Not because life is easier—but because the system learns.

Practice rewires trust.

Presence as Identity

At some point, positivity stops feeling like an approach.

It feels like *you*.

Not as a personality trait, but as a default way of meeting experience. Others may describe you as grounded, calm, or steady—not because you are always composed, but because you recover without hardening.

Presence becomes familiar territory.

The Role of Difficulty in Deepening Practice

Difficulty does not interrupt a lifelong practice.

It refines it.

Each challenge reveals where capacity holds and where it collapses. Each collapse becomes information rather than failure.

Over time, difficulty becomes a teacher rather than an enemy.

Relational Continuity

A lifelong emotional practice is not solitary.

It lives in relationships—in how you listen, repair, set boundaries, and stay engaged.

Others feel the difference not in your words, but in your availability.

Positivity becomes something people experience in your presence.

Why This Practice Matters Now

The modern world rewards speed, certainty, and control.

It rarely rewards presence.

Choosing a lifelong emotional practice is a quiet countercultural act. It prioritizes capacity over performance, coherence over urgency, humanity over efficiency.

This choice does not remove you from the world.

It allows you to meet it without losing yourself.

A Different Measure of Growth

Growth is not measured by how often you are calm.

It is measured by:

- How quickly you notice a contraction
- How gently you return
- How honestly you meet difficulty
- How reliably you remain open

These are subtle metrics.

They are also enduring ones.

Carrying This Forward

You will forget this book.

You will remember pieces of it.

You will lose presence.

You will find it again.

That is the practice.

Positivity lives not in memory, but in return.

A Quiet Closing

This book began by naming an emotional climate that quietly narrows human capacity.

It ends by offering something simple and demanding: a way of living that restores it.

Not through force.

Not through denial.

Not through constant effort.

But through orientation.

Through presence.

Through openness.

Through the willingness to return—again and again.

This is not mastery.

It is a lifelong emotional practice.

And it is enough.

Conclusion

Choosing the Emotional Ground You Stand On

Every life is lived from somewhere.

Not from circumstances alone, not from personality, not from intelligence or intention—but from an emotional ground that shapes how reality is met. This ground is often invisible, yet it determines what we perceive, how we respond, and what becomes possible.

Throughout this book, we have explored that ground.

We have seen how modern life quietly conditions contraction, how negativity becomes a default orientation, how emotional fatigue accumulates, and why intelligence falters when capacity is depleted. We have reframed positivity—not as optimism, denial, or motivation, but as an emotional orientation that restores openness, perception, and choice.

At its heart, this book has made a simple claim:

Emotional intelligence does not fail because people lack skill.

It fails because the emotional ground beneath those skills is unstable.

The Most Important Choice Is Not a Decision

Most choices are visible.

What to say.

What to do.

What path to take?

But the most consequential choice is rarely noticed.

It is the choice of *orientation*—the emotional ground you stand on when life meets you.

You do not usually choose this ground deliberately. It is shaped by habit, pressure, history, and environment. And yet, over time, it becomes the place from which every decision arises.

This is the quiet power of positivity as described in this book.

It is not a reaction to life.

It is the ground from which life is received.

Why This Choice Matters

From a contracted ground:

- Perception narrows
- Reactivity increases
- Effort replaces clarity
- Relationships strain
- Meaning collapses under pressure

From an expanded ground:

- Intelligence becomes accessible
- Regulation is possible
- Empathy is sustainable

- Choice reappears
- Difficulty is met without collapse

The circumstances may be the same.

The experience is not.

Positivity as Responsibility, Not Performance

Choosing your emotional ground is not about being positive *for others*.

It is not about optimism, cheerfulness, or appearing composed.

It is about responsibility—for the state you bring into your own life, your relationships, and the environments you move through.

Because emotional orientation is contagious.

You do not only live from it.

You transmit it.

A Humane Standard

This book has not asked for perfection.

It has not promised constant calm, uninterrupted presence, or emotional mastery.

It has offered something more humane:

- Drift and return

- Contraction and expansion
- Loss of presence and recovery

The practice is not staying open at all times.

The practice is knowing how to come back.

Standing on Different Ground

Life will continue to be demanding.

There will be pressure, uncertainty, loss, conflict, and change. None of this is avoidable.

What *is* available is a different ground beneath your feet.

A ground that allows you to feel deeply without collapsing.

A ground that allows intelligence to function under pressure.

A ground that supports clarity, compassion, and resilience without force.

This ground is not built once.

It is chosen again and again.

A Quiet Invitation

You do not need to remember everything you have read here.

You only need to remember this:

When you notice contraction, fatigue, or reactivity, pause—not to fix yourself, but to reorient.

Ask, quietly:

What ground am I standing on right now?

And if that ground is narrow, harsh, or tense, know this:

You can choose differently.

Not by effort.

Not by denial.

But by returning—to presence, to openness, to the emotional ground that allows you to meet life fully.

This choice will not make life predictable.

It will make it livable.

And that, in the end, is the quiet power of positivity.

POSITIVITY

Pathway to

EMOTIONAL INTELLIGENCE

Appendices

Appendix A — A Simple Positivity Self-Reflection

A brief practice for noticing orientation

This reflection is not a test.

It is not a measure of success or failure.

It is a moment of orientation—an invitation to notice the emotional ground you are standing on *right now*.

Use it whenever you feel off-center, fatigued, reactive, or unclear. It takes only a few minutes and requires no preparation.

Step 1 — Pause the Momentum

Before answering anything, stop for a moment.

Let your body settle where it is.

Notice your breathing without changing it.

Allow the pace of the moment to slow slightly.

This pause is already part of positivity.

Step 2 — Notice Your Current Orientation

Without analyzing, gently reflect on the following prompts. There are no right answers.

- Does my body feel more **tight** or more **open** right now?
- Is my attention narrow and urgent, or wide and available?
- Do I feel more **braced against** what is happening, or **able to meet it**?

Simply notice.

Orientation reveals itself through sensation before thought.

Step 3 — Name the State Without Judgment

Quietly name what you notice, using neutral language:

- I notice contraction.
- I notice vigilance.
- I notice fatigue.
- I notice openness.
- I notice steadiness.

Do not explain.

Do not correct.

Naming without judgment creates space.

Step 4 — Sense Emotional Capacity

Ask yourself gently:

- Do I feel emotionally **resourced, neutral,** or **depleted**?
- Is it easy or effortful to stay present right now?

This is not about blame.

It is about realism.

Capacity determines what is possible.

Step 5 — Invite a Small Shift (Optional)

If you notice contraction or depletion, do not force change.

Instead, invite one small gesture of expansion:

- A slower breath
- Softening the shoulders or jaw
- Letting your gaze widen
- Allowing the next moment to be unhurried

This is not a technique.

It is a permission.

Step 6 — Reorient to Positivity

Quietly ask:

Can I meet the next moment from openness rather than defense—just a little?

If the answer is yes, allow that openness.

If the answer is no, allow that too.

Positivity begins with honesty.

Closing Note

This reflection is meant to be used often and lightly.

Its power comes not from depth, but from repetition.

Each time you notice orientation without judgment, you strengthen your ability to return to expansion. Over time, positivity becomes less of an effort and more of a familiar ground.

You are not trying to feel better.

You are choosing where to stand.

Appendix B — Daily Emotional Check-In Guide

A brief daily practice for orientation and self-trust

This check-in is designed to be simple, repeatable, and non-intrusive.

It is not a mood tracker.

It is not a productivity tool.

It is a way to stay in relationship with your emotional state—without judgment, analysis, or pressure.

Use it once a day, ideally at a consistent time. Two to five minutes is enough.

---

1. Arrive Where You Are

Pause before checking in.

Let your body register that you are stopping.

Notice one physical sensation—feet on the floor, breath in the chest, weight in the chair.

No need to change anything.

Arrival precedes awareness.

---

2. Sense Your Emotional Weather

Ask yourself quietly:

- What is the general emotional tone right now?
- (e.g., steady, tense, flat, open, restless, heavy, calm)

Do not search for precision. One word or image is enough.

Weather changes. It does not define you.

---

3. Notice Your Orientation

Gently reflect:

- Am I meeting today from **openness** or **defensiveness**?
- Do I feel more **available** or **braced**?

This is the heart of the check-in.

Orientation matters more than emotion.

---

4. Assess Emotional Energy

Without judging, ask:

- Is my emotional energy **full**, **moderate**, or **low** today?
- Does engagement feel easy, neutral, or effortful?

This helps align expectations with capacity.

Awareness prevents overextension.

---

5. Name What Is Present

Silently name what you notice:

- I notice pressure.
- I notice fatigue.
- I notice openness.
- I notice uncertainty.

Naming clarifies without amplifying.

---

6. Choose a Gentle Intention

Choose one *orientation-based* intention—not a task.

Examples:

- Move more slowly today.
- Pause before responding.
- Protect emotional energy.
- Stay curious instead of reactive.

Intentions guide state, not performance.

---

7. Close With Permission

End the check-in with a simple acknowledgment:

This is where I am today—and that is allowed.

No fixing.

No improvement plan.

Just honesty.

Using This Guide Over Time

The value of this check-in lies in consistency, not depth.

Over time, you may notice:

- Earlier recognition of contraction
- Greater self-trust
- Shorter recovery after stress
- More stable positivity

This is not emotional control.

It is emotional relationship.

A Final Reminder

You are not checking in to manage yourself.

You are checking in to *meet* yourself.

Positivity grows not from pressure to feel better, but from the habit of returning—day after day—to where you actually are.

Appendix C — Sustaining Positivity Under Pressure

Practical anchors when demands rise

Pressure is not an interruption to emotional practice.

It is where the practice is most needed—and most tested.

This appendix offers grounded guidance for sustaining positivity *during* pressure, not after it passes. These are not techniques to eliminate stress, but anchors that help you remain oriented when demands intensify.

---

1. Redefine Success Under Pressure

Under pressure, success is often defined as performance without visible strain.

This standard is unrealistic—and harmful.

A more sustainable definition is this:

Success under pressure is maintaining openness long enough for intelligence to function.

You may still feel stress.

You may still feel urgency.

You may still feel uncertainty.

What matters is whether you can stay *present* within them.

2. Shorten the Time Horizon

Pressure collapses time.

The mind leaps ahead, forecasting outcomes, consequences, and worst-case scenarios. This creates unnecessary load.

Under pressure:

- Narrow your focus to the *next doable moment*
- Let go of solving the entire situation
- Ask: What is needed now—not later?

Shortening the time horizon reduces threat and restores capacity.

3. Protect Orientation Before Performance

When demands rise, the instinct is to push harder.

Instead, pause briefly to check orientation:

- Am I braced or available?
- Am I rushing or responding?

Even a few seconds of awareness can prevent hours of reactivity.

Orientation determines outcome more reliably than effort.

4. Use the Body as an Ally

Under pressure, the body signals first.

Watch for:

- Tight jaw or shoulders
- Shallow breathing
- Accelerated speech
- Narrowed vision

When these appear, do not criticize yourself.

Simply soften one point of tension or slow one breath.

These small shifts signal safety and prevent escalation.

---

5. Replace Urgency With Pace

Urgency feels necessary—but it often reduces effectiveness.

Pace, by contrast, is deliberate and responsive.

When possible:

- Slow slightly before responding
- Create micro-pauses between tasks
- Speak a bit more slowly than you feel compelled to

This does not reduce productivity.

It increases clarity.

---

6. Separate Pressure From Meaning

Pressure often distorts meaning.

A difficult moment begins to feel like a verdict on competence, worth, or future success.

When this happens, gently remind yourself:

- This is a situation, not my identity.
- This moment does not define the whole.

Restoring context prevents collapse.

---

7. Normalize Contraction—and Return

Even with practice, contraction will happen.

The goal is not to avoid it.

The goal is to *notice and return*.

Each return strengthens resilience.

Each return restores positivity.

Pressure does not mean failure.

It means you are human.

---

8. Choose One Stabilizing Relationship

Under sustained pressure, isolation increases strain.

Identify one person—colleague, friend, or loved one—who allows you to speak without fixing, explaining, or performing.

Being emotionally met restores capacity faster than solving problems alone.

Positivity is supported by connection.

---

9. End the Day With Completion

Pressure often leaves experiences unfinished.

Before sleep, take a moment to acknowledge:

- What was carried today
- What was difficult
- What effort was made

Completion does not require resolution.

It requires acknowledgment.

This allows the nervous system to rest.

Closing Reflection

Sustaining positivity under pressure does not mean staying calm at all times.

It means staying *available*.

Available to notice.

Available to reorient.

Available to respond with intelligence rather than habit.

Pressure will come.

What determines your experience is not how much pressure you face—but whether you know how to return to the emotional ground that supports clarity, resilience, and presence.

That return is always available.

Even—especially—under pressure.

Appendix D — Signals of Expansion and Contraction

How to recognize state before reaction

Before thoughts form and before emotions are named, the body already knows.

Expansion and contraction are not ideas—they are lived states. Learning to recognize their signals early allows you to reorient *before* reactivity takes hold. This appendix offers practical guidance for noticing these signals without judgment.

The goal is not to eliminate contraction.

The goal is to recognize it early and return.

Why Signals Matter

Most emotional reactions feel sudden.

In reality, they are preceded by signals—subtle shifts in the body, breath, attention, and tone. When these signals go unnoticed, contraction deepens and choice disappears.

When they are noticed, space opens.

Recognition is the turning point.

Signals of Contraction

The system preparing to protect

Contraction is a narrowing response. It conserves energy and prepares for threat. These signals are not failures—they are protective cues.

Physical Signals

- Tight jaw, clenched teeth, or pressed lips
- Raised shoulders or collapsed posture
- Shallow, rapid, or held breath
- Tension in chest or stomach
- Reduced bodily sensation (numbness)

Mental Signals

- Urgency or rushing
- Binary thinking (right/wrong, good/bad)
- Replaying conversations or future scenarios
- Fixation on control or certainty
- Difficulty holding nuance or ambiguity

Emotional Signals

- Irritability or impatience
- Defensiveness
- Withdrawal or emotional shutdown
- Heightened sensitivity to tone or feedback
- Feeling easily overwhelmed

Relational Signals

- Listening to respond rather than understand
- Interrupting or overexplaining
- Avoiding contact or difficult conversations
- Interpreting neutral cues as negative

Contraction often feels justified.

It rarely feels chosen.

Signals of Expansion

The system available for engagement

Expansion is an opening response. It allows perception, learning, and connection. Expansion does not require comfort—it requires *safety enough*.

Physical Signals

- Deeper, slower breathing
- Softer muscle tone
- Upright yet relaxed posture
- Greater bodily awareness
- Ease of movement

Mental Signals

- Wider attention
- Ability to hold multiple perspectives
- Curiosity about what is happening
- Reduced urgency
- Clearer thinking without force

Emotional Signals

- Emotional responsiveness without flooding
- Capacity to feel without escalation
- Patience

- Emotional steadiness
- Quiet confidence

Relational Signals

- Genuine listening
- Comfort with pauses or silence
- Willingness to repair or clarify
- Warmth without effort
- Presence felt by others

Expansion often feels subtle.

It is quieter than contraction—but far more powerful.

A Crucial Distinction

Expansion does **not** mean:

- Feeling happy
- Being calm at all times
- Liking what is happening
- Agreeing or approving

You can feel grief, fear, or anger *in expansion*.

What matters is not the emotion—but whether the system remains open.

Using These Signals in Daily Life

You do not need to track all signals.

Choose one or two that are most familiar to you:

- Breath
- Jaw tension
- Mental urgency
- Listening quality

These become your early indicators.

When you notice contraction:

- Do not fix
- Do not judge
- Do not explain

Simply acknowledge: "I notice contraction."

That acknowledgment alone begins reorientation.

Why This Appendix Matters

Positivity does not begin with thinking differently.

It begins with *noticing state*.

When you can recognize expansion and contraction early, emotional intelligence stops being reactive and becomes responsive. You gain access to choice—not because life is easier, but because you see sooner.

A Final Reminder

Contraction will happen.

Expansion will fade.

Return will be required.

This is not a flaw in the practice.

It *is* the practice.

Recognize.

Reorient.

Return.

Again and again.

Appendix E — Positivity vs. Emotional Bypassing

Staying open without avoiding reality

Positivity is often rejected because it has been confused with avoidance.

When positivity is used to smooth over discomfort, deny pain, or rush toward meaning before experience is met, it becomes emotionally dishonest. People sense this instinctively—and resist it.

This appendix clarifies the difference between genuine positivity and emotional bypassing, so openness is not achieved at the cost of truth.

What Emotional Bypassing Is

Emotional bypassing occurs when language, belief, or intention is used to *avoid* feeling what is present.

It is not usually conscious. It often comes from a desire to cope, to stay functional, or to be "healthy."

Bypassing does not resolve emotion.

It delays it.

Common Signs of Emotional Bypassing

You may be bypassing when:

- You move to explanation before emotion is felt
- You search for meaning while the body is still braced
- You minimize your own experience to appear resilient
- You use positive language to silence discomfort
- You feel calm on the surface but tense underneath

Bypassing often feels composed.

The body, however, remains contracted.

Language That Signals Bypassing

Bypassing often sounds reassuring—but leaves something unacknowledged.

Examples:

- "Everything happens for a reason."
- "I shouldn't feel this way."
- "It could be worse."
- "I'm fine, really."
- "I just need to stay positive."

These statements may be true *eventually*.

They are unhelpful *too early*.

What True Positivity Is

True positivity does not leap ahead of experience.

It begins by *meeting what is here*—without denial, urgency, or correction.

True positivity says:

- "This is hard, and I can stay with it."
- "I don't have clarity yet."
- "I can allow this feeling without acting from it."
- "Openness matters more than feeling good."

This form of positivity increases capacity rather than overriding emotion.

The Key Difference

The difference between bypassing and positivity is **timing**.

- Bypassing moves upward too fast
- Positivity moves *through* experience

Bypassing skips sensation.

Positivity includes it.

Why Bypassing Backfires

When emotion is bypassed:

- The nervous system remains activated
- Emotional energy stays trapped
- Reactions resurface later—often stronger
- Trust in self-awareness erodes

People may appear regulated while becoming increasingly fatigued or disconnected.

Positivity and Emotional Honesty

Positivity without honesty is brittle.

Honesty does not require intensity.

It requires presence.

- You can acknowledge pain quietly.
- You can feel uncertainty without dramatizing it.
- You can be open without knowing what it means yet.

This honesty stabilizes the system.

A Simple Check-In

When you notice yourself reaching for positivity, ask:

- Have I allowed myself to feel this yet?
- Is my body open—or still braced?
- Am I trying to feel better, or to be present?

These questions prevent bypassing without effort.

Why This Appendix Matters

Many people abandon positivity because they associate it with dishonesty.

This appendix restores its integrity.

Positivity, as defined in this book, does not avoid pain.

It prevents collapse *within* pain.

A Closing Reminder

You do not need to rise above experience.

You need to *meet* it.

When experience is met fully, perspective reorganizes naturally.

That is not bypassing.

That is genuine positivity.

Appendix F — A One-Minute Reset Practice

A rapid return to presence when time is scarce

This practice is designed for real life.

It is for moments when pressure is high, time is limited, and regulation feels out of reach.

It does not require privacy, stillness, or special conditions.

It takes about one minute.

Its purpose is not to make you calm.

Its purpose is to help you *return*.

When to Use This Reset

Use this practice:

- Before responding to something charged
- When you feel rushed or reactive
- Between tasks or conversations
- When you notice contraction or fatigue

You do not need to wait until you are overwhelmed.

Early use makes it more effective.

The One-Minute Reset

1. Pause (10 seconds)

Stop what you are doing—just briefly.

Let your body register the pause.

Do not analyze.

Do not change anything yet.

Pausing interrupts momentum.

---

2. Exhale Fully (10–15 seconds)

Let one or two slow, complete exhales leave the body.

Do not force the inhale.

Let it return on its own.

Longer exhales signal safety.

---

3. Name the State (10 seconds)

Quietly name what you notice:

- "I notice urgency."
- "I notice contraction."
- "I notice fatigue."

Use neutral language.

Naming brings awareness online.

---

4. Widen Attention (15–20 seconds)

Gently widen your awareness:

- Notice the space around your body
- Feel your feet or seat
- Let your gaze soften or widen

Widening counters narrowing.

---

5. Re-enter with Orientation (10–15 seconds)

Before continuing, ask:

"How do I want to meet the next moment?"

Choose an orientation—not a behavior:

- Slower
- Clearer
- More open
- Less urgent

Then continue.

What This Practice Does

This reset:

- Interrupts reactivity
- Restores minimal expansion
- Returns access to intelligence
- Preserves emotional energy

It does not solve problems.

It changes *state*.

If One Minute Feels Like Too Much

On very difficult days, simplify:

- Pause
- Exhale once
- Notice you are contracted

That is enough.

Return happens in layers.

Why This Practice Works

Negativity loops depend on speed and narrowing.

This reset introduces:

- Slowness
- Awareness
- Widening

That combination is enough to break the loop.

A Final Note

This practice is not a technique to master.

It is a permission to interrupt.

Each time you use it, you reinforce a new pattern:

I can return without force.

Over time, that knowing becomes embodied.

And presence becomes more available—one minute at a time.

Appendix G — Positivity and Emotional Boundaries

Remaining open without overextension

Positivity does not require emotional openness without limits.

In fact, without boundaries, positivity becomes unsustainable. Openness turns into overexposure.

Care turns into depletion. Presence turns into pressure.

This appendix clarifies how emotional boundaries *protect* positivity rather than oppose it—allowing you to remain open, responsive, and human without exhausting yourself.

What Emotional Boundaries Really Are

Emotional boundaries are not walls.

They are internal reference points that help you distinguish:

- What you are responsible for
- What belongs to someone else
- Where your emotional energy ends

Boundaries create *containment*, not distance.

They allow connection to occur without collapse.

Why Boundaries Are Often Misunderstood

Many people equate boundaries with withdrawal, coldness, or selfishness.

As a result, they avoid setting them—and pay the price in fatigue, resentment, or emotional shutdown.

True boundaries do not reduce care.

They make care sustainable.

Positivity Without Boundaries Becomes Strain

When boundaries are weak:

- Empathy turns into absorption
- Availability turns into obligation
- Listening turns into carrying
- Helping turns into rescuing

The system begins to contract—not because connection is wrong, but because capacity is exceeded.

Positivity requires enough space to breathe.

Boundaries as an Expression of Positivity

Healthy boundaries are a sign of expansion.

They arise from clarity, not defensiveness.

You can say:

- "I'm not available for this right now."

- "I need to pause this conversation."
- "I care, and I can't take this on."

without anger, guilt, or withdrawal.

Boundaries stated from presence feel firm and respectful.

Internal Boundaries Come First

External boundaries are only effective when internal boundaries are clear.

Internal boundaries involve noticing:

- When emotional energy drops
- When resentment appears
- When urgency replaces willingness
- When care feels heavy rather than open

These signals indicate the need for reorientation—not self-criticism.

Staying Open While Saying No

Saying no does not require closing your heart.

You can remain emotionally open while limiting engagement.

This is the difference between:

- *Withdrawal* (closing down)
- *Boundary* (staying present while limiting)

Positivity allows no to be spoken without rupture.

Why Guilt Appears

Guilt often arises when boundaries challenge old conditioning:

- Being responsible for others' emotions
- Being available at all times
- Avoiding disappointment or conflict

This guilt does not mean the boundary is wrong.

It means a pattern is changing.

Stay present. Let guilt pass without acting from it.

Boundaries and Self-Trust

Each time you honor an emotional boundary, trust deepens.

You learn that:

- You will listen to your own limits
- You do not need to collapse to connect
- Presence does not require sacrifice

Self-trust strengthens positivity.

A Simple Boundary Check

When unsure, ask:

- Is this coming from openness or obligation?
- Do I feel willing—or pressured?
- Will saying yes contract or expand me?

The body often answers before the mind.

Why This Appendix Matters

Without boundaries, positivity becomes another demand.

With boundaries, positivity becomes livable.

You can remain open without being drained.

You can care without carrying.

You can stay present without disappearing.

A Closing Reflection

Boundaries are not a retreat from relationship.

They are what make relationship possible—over time.

Positivity does not ask you to give endlessly.

It asks you to remain *available*.

And availability requires space.

Appendix H — Personal Positivity Inventory

A reflective assessment for awareness—not evaluation

This inventory is not a test.

It does not produce a score.

It is not designed to measure how "positive" you are.

Its purpose is to help you notice patterns—where expansion comes naturally, where contraction appears, and what supports or drains your emotional orientation.

Use this inventory periodically, not daily. Quarterly or seasonally is often enough.

Answer honestly, without judgment.

How to Use This Inventory

- Read each prompt slowly
- Respond in writing or reflection
- Notice sensations as well as thoughts
- Do not try to improve your answers

Awareness is the outcome.

Section 1 — Baseline Orientation

1. In most ordinary days, I tend to meet life from:

- o ☐ Openness
- o ☐ Neutral steadiness
- o ☐ Vigilance or defensiveness

2. I most often notice contraction when:
   - o ☐ I feel rushed
   - o ☐ I feel evaluated
   - o ☐ I feel uncertain
   - o ☐ I feel emotionally responsible for others
   - o ☐ Other: ___________________

3. Expansion tends to arise for me when:
   - o ☐ I slow down
   - o ☐ I feel understood
   - o ☐ I am in nature or quiet
   - o ☐ I feel meaningful engagement
   - o ☐ Other: ___________________

Section 2 — Emotional Energy and Recovery

4. My emotional energy is most often depleted by:
   - o ☐ Prolonged pressure
   - o ☐ Unresolved conversations
   - o ☐ Overcommitment
   - o ☐ Emotional absorption
   - o ☐ Self-criticism

5. I tend to recover best when I:
   - o ☐ Rest physically
   - o ☐ Have unstructured time
   - o ☐ Feel emotionally met
   - o ☐ Allow emotions to surface

- o ☐ Reduce demand
6. I notice that I delay recovery when I:
    - o ☐ Push through fatigue
    - o ☐ Minimize my own experience
    - o ☐ Stay busy to avoid feeling
    - o ☐ Expect myself to bounce back quickly

Section 3 — Positivity Under Pressure

7. Under pressure, my default response is to:
    - o ☐ Accelerate
    - o ☐ Control
    - o ☐ Withdraw
    - o ☐ Overthink
    - o ☐ Stay present
8. When pressure is sustained, I notice:
    - o ☐ Reduced patience
    - o ☐ Narrowed thinking
    - o ☐ Emotional flatness
    - o ☐ Heightened reactivity
    - o ☐ Loss of clarity
9. What helps me most under pressure is:
    - o ☐ Slowing pace
    - o ☐ Clarifying priorities
    - o ☐ Being emotionally met
    - o ☐ Creating space before responding

Section 4 — Relationships and Boundaries

10. In relationships, I am most likely to lose positivity when:
    - ○ ☐ Conflict arises
    - ○ ☐ Expectations are unclear
    - ○ ☐ I feel misunderstood
    - ○ ☐ I overextend emotionally
11. I maintain openness best when I:
    - ○ ☐ Set boundaries early
    - ○ ☐ Name what I'm feeling
    - ○ ☐ Pause before responding
    - ○ ☐ Allow silence
12. I know a boundary is needed when I feel:
    - ○ ☐ Resentment
    - ○ ☐ Fatigue
    - ○ ☐ Urgency
    - ○ ☐ Loss of choice

Section 5 — Self-Relationship

13. When I notice my own contraction, I usually:
    - ○ ☐ Judge myself
    - ○ ☐ Try to fix it
    - ○ ☐ Ignore it
    - ○ ☐ Become curious
    - ○ ☐ Allow it
14. The tone I most often take with myself is:
    - ○ ☐ Kind
    - ○ ☐ Neutral
    - ○ ☐ Demanding

- o ☐ Critical

15. I return to presence most easily when I:
    - o ☐ Acknowledge where I am
    - o ☐ Reduce self-pressure
    - o ☐ Breathe or pause
    - o ☐ Stop trying to improve

Closing Reflection

Complete the following gently:

- One pattern I am beginning to notice is:

- One way I could support positivity more realistically is:

- One place where I am already doing better than I think is:

A Final Note

This inventory is not meant to change you.

It is meant to *show you*.

When patterns are seen clearly and kindly, orientation shifts naturally.

Positivity does not grow through evaluation.

It grows through awareness, honesty, and return.

Appendix I — A 14-Day Positivity Integration Path

A gentle daily rhythm for embodiment

This integration path is not a challenge, a program, or a discipline.

It is a **light daily orientation**—a way of living with the ideas of this book long enough for them to move from understanding into experience.

Each day offers a single focus.

No exercises are required. No outcomes are expected.

Simply let the theme inform how you notice the day.

How to Use This Path

- Spend 1–2 minutes each morning reading the day's focus
- Let it sit in the background of your awareness
- Notice moments—not performance
- If you miss a day, continue without restarting

This is integration, not compliance.

Day 1 — Orientation

Focus: Notice the emotional ground you stand on today.

- Am I meeting the day from openness or vigilance?
- What does my body tell me before my thoughts do?

No change required.

Only noticing.

Day 2 — The Body Knows

Focus: Track physical signals of expansion and contraction.

- Breath
- Jaw
- Shoulders
- Pace

The body reveals state faster than the mind.

Day 3 — Slowing Without Stopping

Focus: Introduce small slowness.

- Slower steps
- Slower speech
- Fewer rushed transitions

Slowing restores perception.

Day 4 — Self-Judgment Awareness

Focus: Notice the tone you take with yourself.

- Is it corrective or curious?
- Demanding or kind?

Self-awareness deepens when judgment softens.

Day 5 — Regulation Without Resistance

Focus: Allow emotion without fixing.

- Let feelings move
- Stay present without explanation

Non-resistance restores stability.

Day 6 — Emotional Energy

Focus: Notice where energy flows—and where it drains.

- What gives energy today?
- What quietly depletes it?

Capacity determines positivity.

Day 7 — Recovery

Focus: Allow completion at the end of the day.

- Acknowledge effort
- Name what was difficult
- Let the day close

Completion enables rest.

Day 8 — Boundaries

Focus: Notice where boundaries are needed.

- Where does willingness end?
- Where does obligation begin?

Boundaries protect openness.

Day 9 — Empathy Without Absorption

Focus: Stay present without carrying.

- Listen fully
- Stay grounded
- Let others own their experience

Empathy does not require self-loss.

Day 10 — Emotional Tone

Focus: Notice the tone you bring into interactions.

- Rushed or settled?
- Defensive or open?

Tone communicates before words.

Day 11 — Pressure

Focus: Observe how pressure changes your state.

- Do you speed up?
- Do you narrow?

Return to orientation before action.

Day 12 — Uncertainty

Focus: Allow not knowing.

- Resist premature certainty
- Stay available to emergence

Tolerance for uncertainty preserves clarity.

Day 13 — Reframing Through Expansion

Focus: Let meaning reorganize naturally.

- Notice what changes when perception widens
- Do not force interpretation

Reframing follows regulation.

Day 14 — Integration

Focus: Reflect gently.

- What feels more familiar now?
- What returns more easily?
- Where is positivity quieter—but steadier?

Integration happens without effort.

After the 14 Days

You may repeat this path.

You may linger on certain days.

You may forget it entirely—and return later.

That is the practice.

A Closing Reminder

Positivity does not arrive all at once.

It integrates slowly, through lived moments, quiet noticing, and repeated return.

This path does not teach you something new.

It helps you *remember* where you already know how to stand.

Appendix J — Language That Supports Expansion

Words that stabilize rather than escalate

Language does more than communicate information.

It shapes emotional state.

The words we choose—especially under pressure—either widen perception or narrow it. They can calm nervous systems or activate them, create space or collapse it.

This appendix offers language that supports **expansion**—in yourself and in others—by reducing threat and restoring openness.

This is not about saying the "right" thing.

It is about choosing language that matches the orientation you want to create.

Why Language Matters

Under contraction, language becomes sharp, urgent, and absolute.

Under expansion, language becomes spacious, specific, and grounded.

People respond to tone and implication before content.

Language is one of the fastest ways to shift emotional climate.

Language That Narrows (and Why)

The following types of language tend to increase contraction—
especially under stress.

Urgency Language

- "We need this now."
- "There's no time."
- "This has to be done immediately."

Urgency collapses time and reduces clarity.

Absolutist Language

- "This always happens."
- "You never listen."
- "There's only one option."

Absolutes narrow perception and provoke defensiveness.

Evaluative Language

- "That was wrong."
- "You should know better."
- "This is unacceptable."

Evaluation activates threat before understanding.

Language That Supports Expansion

Expansion-supportive language reduces threat while preserving honesty and accountability.

Pacing Language

- "Let's slow this down for a moment."
- "We don't need to resolve everything right now."
- "Let's take this one step at a time."

Pacing restores time.

Orientation Language

- "What's most important here?"
- "What are we responding to right now?"
- "What's actually being asked of us?"

Orientation clarifies without pressure.

Curiosity Language

- "Can you help me understand?"
- "What are we missing?"
- "What's your experience of this?"

Curiosity widens perception.

Containment Language

- "This is difficult—and manageable."
- "We can hold this without rushing."
- "We don't need to fix this immediately."

Containment signals safety.

Boundary Language

- "I'm not available for this right now."
- "Let's pause this conversation."
- "I need a moment before responding."

Boundaries maintain openness without collapse.

Language for Self-Talk

The language you use internally matters as much as what you say aloud.

Contracting Self-Talk

- "I shouldn't feel this way."
- "I need to get it together."
- "This is too much."

This language adds pressure to pressure.

Expanding Self-Talk

- "This is hard—and I can stay present."
- "I can slow down."

- "I don't need clarity yet."

Self-talk sets internal tone.

When Words Matter Most

Language is most powerful:

- During conflict
- Under pressure
- In leadership roles
- In moments of uncertainty
- When emotions are elevated

In these moments, *how* something is said matters more than *what* is said.

Using This Appendix Practically

Choose one or two phrases that feel natural to you.

Practice using them:

- In difficult conversations
- During internal stress
- When slowing a situation down

Do not aim for perfection.

Aim for presence.

A Final Reflection

Language does not need to be clever or comforting.

It needs to be true without being threatening.

When language supports expansion, intelligence returns.

Not because problems disappear—but because people can meet them without collapsing.

That is the quiet power of words that widen rather than rush.

Appendix K — Positivity in Leadership Conversations

Holding clarity, authority, and openness at the same time

Leadership conversations shape more than outcomes.

They shape emotional climate.

Before content is heard, the nervous systems involved register tone, pace, and intention. Positivity in leadership conversations is not about being agreeable or soft—it is about creating the conditions in which honesty, intelligence, and responsibility can function.

This appendix offers guidance for bringing positivity—understood as emotional orientation—into conversations where stakes are high.

Before the Conversation: Check Orientation

Before entering an important conversation, pause briefly and ask:

- Am I regulated enough to listen?
- Am I carrying urgency or clarity?
- Am I seeking understanding—or control?

This check does not delay leadership.

It strengthens it.

Orientation determines outcome.

Set the Emotional Frame Early

How a conversation opens matters.

A few grounding words can stabilize the entire exchange:

- "Let's slow this down and think together."
- "This is important—we don't need to rush it."
- "I want to understand before we decide."

These statements do not lower standards.

They widen capacity.

Separate Issues From Identity

Under pressure, feedback can easily feel personal.

Positivity maintains this distinction:

- Address behavior or outcomes—not character
- Name impact without assigning blame
- Keep dignity intact

Language such as:

- "This outcome doesn't meet the requirement."
- "Here's what isn't working yet."

supports accountability without threat.

Use Curiosity Before Conclusion

When something is unclear or problematic, curiosity preserves expansion:

- "Help me understand how this happened."
- "What were you responding to at the time?"
- "What constraints were present?"

Curiosity is not weakness.

It is information-gathering.

Regulate Pace Under Escalation

When emotions rise, pace becomes more important than content.

If you notice:

- Faster speech
- Interruptions
- Defensive tone

Pause deliberately.

You might say:

- "Let's take a moment."
- "I want to be careful here."

Slowing pace restores intelligence.

Hold Authority Without Hardening

Positivity allows authority without intimidation.

You can be clear and firm while remaining open:

- "This decision stands."
- "This expectation remains."
- "We will address this."

Said from presence, firmness stabilizes rather than threatens.

Allow Silence

Silence is often uncomfortable—but powerful.

In expansion:

- Silence allows processing
- Silence invites reflection
- Silence reduces escalation

Resist the urge to fill every gap.

Silence supports insight.

Repair When Needed

Even with skill, conversations can misstep.

Repair does not require perfection—only presence:

- "I realize my tone tightened earlier."
- "Let me say that more clearly."
- "I want to reset this."

Repair restores trust faster than explanation.

Close With Orientation, Not Just Action

How a conversation ends matters.

Before closing, reinforce stability:

- "We're aligned on next steps."
- "We'll revisit this once there's more information."
- "This is workable."

Orientation at the close carries forward.

Why This Appendix Matters

Leadership conversations often fail not because of poor decisions, but because emotional climate collapses under pressure.

Positivity prevents that collapse.

It allows leaders to:

- Hold complexity
- Maintain authority
- Invite responsibility
- Preserve dignity

All at once.

A Final Note to Leaders

You do not need to manage emotions.

You need to manage *state*—your own first.

When your orientation is open, others feel it.

And when people feel it, conversations become places where intelligence can actually function.

That is positivity in leadership—not as style, but as substance.

Appendix L — When Positivity Is Not Available

Meeting depletion with honesty

There will be times when positivity feels unreachable.

No amount of reflection helps. Openness feels distant. Even the idea of expansion sounds unrealistic. These moments can be unsettling—especially if you have come to value presence and emotional clarity.

This appendix exists for those times.

Not to correct them.

Not to reframe them.

But to meet them honestly.

Recognizing Depletion Without Judgment

When positivity is not available, the system is usually depleted—not resistant.

Signs of depletion include:

- Emotional flatness or numbness
- Irritability without clear cause
- Loss of curiosity
- Heightened sensitivity
- Feeling "done" rather than distressed

These are not failures of practice.

They are signals that capacity is low.

Why Forcing Positivity Backfires

Trying to restore positivity through effort creates additional pressure.

Statements like:

- "I should be able to handle this."
- "I know better than this."
- "I just need to reframe."

increase contraction.

The nervous system does not respond to instruction when depleted.

It responds to safety.

What Is Available When Positivity Is Not

Even when positivity is unavailable, some capacities remain.

You may not be able to expand—but you can:

- Acknowledge depletion
- Reduce demand
- Avoid self-judgment
- Choose not to escalate

These are not small things.

They prevent further loss.

Permission Is the First Return

The most important shift in depletion is permission.

Permission to:

- Be where you are
- Not understand yet
- Not fix anything
- Not perform emotionally

This permission stabilizes the system enough for recovery to begin.

Lowering the Bar Intentionally

In depletion, adjust expectations consciously.

- Do less, not more
- Speak less if needed
- Delay decisions when possible
- Choose containment over openness

Lowering the bar is not avoidance.

It is intelligent pacing.

Containment Before Expansion

Positivity requires capacity.

When capacity is low, aim for containment—not expansion.

Containment means:

- Staying grounded
- Preventing emotional spillover
- Protecting energy
- Maintaining basic regulation

Expansion will return later.

The Role of Being Met

Depletion often deepens in isolation.

If possible, seek one person who can:

- Listen without fixing
- Be present without expectation
- Allow silence

Being emotionally met restores capacity faster than insight.

Trust the Rhythm

Emotional life is cyclical.

Expansion fades.

Contraction appears.

Depletion follows strain.

Renewal returns.

Trying to flatten this rhythm creates suffering.

Honoring it restores trust.

A Gentle Reminder

You are not meant to be open all the time.

Positivity is not constant availability.

It is the ability to return—when returning is possible.

And when it is not, to wait without self-attack.

Closing Reflection

When positivity is unavailable, do not ask:

"How do I get back?"

Ask instead:

"What does my system need right now?"

Often, the answer is not expansion—but rest, containment, or simple acknowledgment.

That answer is enough.

Positivity will return—not because you force it, but because you respected the moment when it could not.

Appendix M — A Closing Reflection for Ongoing Practice

Returning, again and again

This book does not end with a solution.

It ends with a rhythm.

A rhythm of noticing and returning, of expansion and contraction, of presence lost and found. This rhythm is not something to overcome. It is the nature of emotional life.

This closing reflection is an invitation to carry that rhythm forward—without pressure, ambition, or expectation.

What This Practice Is—and Is Not

This practice is not:

- A requirement to stay calm
- A mandate to be positive
- A standard to live up to

It is not a performance.

This practice *is*:

- A willingness to notice state
- A capacity to return without judgment
- A way of standing on emotional ground that supports clarity

The Only Question That Matters

Over time, many questions fall away.

What remains is simple:

Where am I standing right now?

Not:

- Am I doing this correctly?
- Am I calm enough?
- Am I better than before?

Just:

- Am I contracted or open?
- Am I braced or available?

This question never judges.

It orients.

Return Is the Practice

You will lose presence.

You will rush.

You will contract.

You will react.

These moments are not interruptions.

They are invitations.

Each return strengthens trust—not in technique, but in your capacity to reorient.

Progress You Cannot Measure

The deepest changes are subtle.

You may notice:

- Quicker awareness of contraction
- Less self-criticism
- Shorter recovery after stress
- Greater honesty with yourself
- A quieter steadiness

These changes cannot be forced.

They emerge when the practice is gentle.

Let the Practice Change Shape

This practice will evolve.

What helps now may not help later.

What once felt grounding may feel unnecessary.

Allow the practice to change.

Rigidity contracts.

Adaptation expands.

Carry This Into Relationship

Others will feel your practice.

Not because you speak about it, but because of:

- How you listen
- How you pause
- How you respond under pressure
- How you repair when needed

Presence transmits.

When You Forget

You will forget this book.

That is expected.

When you do, nothing is lost.

The practice lives not in memory, but in the moment you notice you are not present—and choose to return.

A Quiet Closing

There is nothing more to add.

No final instruction.

No promise of mastery.

Only this:

Stand where openness is possible.

Return when you leave it.

Be patient with the rhythm.

That is the lifelong practice. And it is enough.